"*Swimming Studies* sets out, through a fusion of words and pictures, to capture a bittersweet part of the writer's past as completely as a scent trapped in a bottle. The book is beautiful as both a story and an object. It's about being very, very good at something, when you want to be great. I was moved by it in ways both expected and unexpected."   —John Jeremiah Sullivan, author of *Pulphead*

"If there is a more beautifully observed examination of weightlessness, silence, rigor, and delight of what it means to swim, I've never read it. Leanne Shapton is one of the most broadly creative and gifted people at work today; a true artist, both visual and verbal. There seems to be nothing she cannot write or paint about: adolescence, Canada, yearning, dawn—even cake, for heaven's sake!— with a precision both surgical and poetic. The joys of *Swimming Studies* are in being in the care of someone of a prodigious and protean mind. My talent crush is official and deep."
                    —David Rakoff, author of *Half Empty*

"I'm so happy this book exists. *Swimming Studies* expresses what it's like to be haunted by the person one used to be, and the search for how that person exists in the present. Leanne Shapton writes with such curiosity, ruefulness, intelligence, and grace. Here we see how the discipline of being an athlete can condition one's way of making art, and how the patience necessary to make art teaches other types of patience. Like the patience required to be a spouse and to love a person always. This book is a rare treat for anyone who cares about any of these things."
                    —Sheila Heti, author of *How Should a Person Be?*

"A cool memoir about competitive swimming that might as well be called *The Unbearable Lightness of Being*. . . . Shapton, never self-pitying, offers an original, mythical elixir of life in the water."
—*Newsweek*

"[A] thoughtful, exquisitely written book . . . ostensibly about [Shapton's] lifelong relationship to the sport, complete with photos of her various bathing suits and meditations on the difference between swimming (i.e., competitive swimming) and bathing (i.e., swimming for fun). . . . She even includes some haunting, cobalt blue illustrations of pools she frequents as an adult, as well as a color guide to different swimming smells, such as 'coach: fresh laundry, windbreaker nylon, Mennen Speed Stick, Magic Marker, and bologna.' These extra visual elements dazzle, but the specifics of this world and her insightful take on her own far-from-ordinary life are what makes any reader wonder if Shapton's gold medal might have already been won—in writing."   —Oprah.com, Book of the Week

"Shapton draws on her experience training for the Olympic trials in a refreshing and thoughtful memoir about swimming as competition and way of life. Her ode to the water is not only philosophical but incredibly moving."   —*Entertainment Weekly*

"The talented illustrator Leanne Shapton, in her pointillistic and quietly profound new memoir, *Swimming Studies* . . . writes as confidently as she draws, and memorably conjures swimming's intense, primordial and isolating pleasures. . . . Shapton's prose frequently has the density of poetry. . . . [She] is so smart and so likable that you will pass her book along to the swimmers in your life."
—Dwight Garner, *The New York Times*

"In this small, lovely book, [Shapton] combines words and images in an exquisitely observed meditation on swimming and memory. . . . What's thrilling about this book is its author's careful attention to detail and unlikely beauty. More impressionistic than a traditional memoir, the book nonetheless sketches an arc that brings the author back to competitive swimming, in masters races in the United States."   —Kate Tuttle, *The Boston Globe*

"A fusion of cool, clear-eyed prose and watercolors, photographs and painted portraits . . . [and] a curiously arresting study of the transition from a world of rigor and routine to one of reflection and recreation. . . . The brilliance of *Swimming Studies* lies in its delicate exploration of how the identities we've carved out for ourselves in the present are both haunted and shaped by the people we used to be."   —*Time Out New York*

"[W]hat makes this book astounding . . . [is] any dedicated swimmer knows exactly what Shapton means; we sense and control our movements, from the tips of our fingers to the flutter of our feet, breathing very specifically, detecting any shifts in conditions, from the presence of other swimmers to the tug of a current. . . . Shapton pares down her experiences as a swimmer and grafts the core lessons to other parts of her life, allowing them to bloom in ways that have everything and nothing to do with swimming."
          —Buzz Poole, TheMillions.com

"Painter and illustrator Leanne Shapton relates with poignancy the details of a competitive swimmer's life . . . beautifully written, beautifully constructed, and thoughtful."   —*The Huffington Post*

"[*Swimming Studies*] is brilliant, eccentric and moving—an immersion in a life. . . . Shapton has a novelist's instinct for the nostalgic charge of the inconsequential. . . . Her language is as crisp as the autumn day she describes."   —Kate Kellaway, *The Observer* (UK)

"Acknowledging the ultimate incomprehensibility of athletic greatness, [Shapton] nonetheless brings us closer to its essence. . . . If those countless practice laps and those not-quite-Olympian results were what it took to produce *Swimming Studies*, it was worth it: Shapton has bottled the elusive meaning of having tried and failed at a sport better than any book I've read since Pat Jordan's classic *A False Spring*. Read *Swimming Studies* and enjoy the incomprehensible greatness of the world's best all the more."

—Ian McGillis, *Montreal Gazette* (Canada)

"[Shapton's] eye for detail [is] amazingly shrewd. . . . Gaspingly beautiful in its insight, proving her project actually has very little to do with swimming . . . *Swimming Studies* is an intimate and beautiful meditation on human fallibility and the embarrassing, often unstated anxiety of success."

—Stacey May Fowles, *National Post* (Canada)

"In her illustrated memoir, Shapton, a writer, artist, and former contender for the Canadian Olympic team, grapples with the habits she learned as a teen-age competitive swimmer . . . and her honed attention to detail gives the reader the sensation of watching a meticulous mind watching itself, down to the hundredth of a second."

—*The New Yorker*

"It looks like Shapton can succeed at whatever she puts her mind to; swimming is where that started. . . . As few people can, Shapton draws a connection between making art and being an athlete, focusing on the unending effort it takes to do well. . . . She is, no doubt, a creative powerhouse, one who puts words and pictures together with a quiet force that comes only from solid, dedicated practice." —Carolyn Kellogg, *Los Angeles Times*

"I was a competitive swimmer, and I have never read anything that captured the sport so well. Shapton knows just the details to include. . . . Her sparse, satisfying prose is your guide, and you're glad to get to swim beside her."
—Carolyn Kormann, TheNewYorker.com

"Through immaculate observation and evocative recollection, Leanne Shapton's autobiographical *Swimming Studies* achieves the seemingly impossible. In a series of sharp snapshots of life as a competitive swimmer and beyond, she has managed to find 'the language of belonging,' giving a voice to silent hours spent submerged in water. . . . Beautifully written and gorgeous to look at, too. . . . Ultimately, *Swimming Studies* is about more than swimming. It's about how the discipline of competitive sport teaches routine, perseverance and good habits. It's about how the diligence of athletic practice can translate into art, communication and even love." —Nicola Joyce, *The Washington Post*

SWIMMING
STUDIES

LEANNE SHAPTON

BLUE RIDER PRESS *New York*

blue
rider
press

An imprint of Penguin Random House LLC
375 Hudson Street
New York, New York 10014

Copyright © 2012 by Leanne Shapton
Photographs in "Size" copyright © 2012 by Michael Schmelling

Blue Rider Press is a registered trademark and its colophon is a trademark of
Penguin Random House LLC.

"Swimming Studies" originally appeared on nytimes.com, as did portions of
"Derek" and "Night Kitchen," the latter two in pieces originally titled
"In the Night Kitchen" and "Raiders of the Night Kitchen."

The Library of Congress has catalogued the hardcover edition as follows:

Shapton, Leanne.
Swimming studies / Leanne Shapton.
p.   cm.
ISBN 978-0-399-15817-9 (hardcover)
1. Shapton, Leanne.   2. Women swimmers—Canada—Biography.   I. Title.
GV838.S47A3   2012   2012011506
797.21092—dc23
[B]

Blue Rider Press hardcover edition: July 2012
Blue Rider Press paperback edition: May 2016
Blue Rider Press paperback ISBN: 978-0-399-17484-1

Printed in the United States of America
1   3   5   7   9   10   8   6   4   2

Book design by Claire Naylon Vaccaro and Leanne Shapton

Some personal names and identifying details have been changed.

To Mom, Dad, and Derek

CONTENTS

SWIMMING STUDIES

WATER

Water is elemental, it's what we're made of, what we can't live within or without. Trying to define what swimming means to me is like looking at a shell sitting in a few feet of clear, still water. There it is, in sharp focus, but once I reach for it, breaking the surface, the ripples refract the shell. It becomes five shells, twenty-five shells, some smaller, some larger, and I blindly feel for what I saw perfectly before trying to grasp it.

QUITTING

Say I'm swimming with people, in the ocean, a pool, or a lake, and one of them knows about my history as a swimmer, and remarks to the others, "Leanne's an Olympic swimmer." I'll protest: "No, no, I only went as far as the Olympic trials— I didn't go to the Olympics." But the boast bobs up like a balloon, bright and curious to some, wistful and exposed to me.

When pressed, it is usually enough to say I went to the 1988 and 1992 Canadian Olympic trials. That nationally, I was ranked eighth once, briefly. I explain that to go to the Olympics you have to finish first or second at the trials. This is where the conversations end. After paddling around we wade into the shallows or hoist ourselves up onto the boat or the dock, and the conversation turns toward food, or gossip.

I don't have vivid memories of the Olympic trials, or of winning medals; I barely remember quitting the first time, in 1989, or how I told Mitch, my coach. It would have probably been at an evening practice. On the deck, after, when the other swimmers had gone to change. I would have been standing there in my suit with my duffel bag and towel. He would have said something like "What's up?" And then I would have said it. Said my family was moving to the countryside, said I did not want to live with another family in order to train—so, I said, I had decided to quit.

I might have done it while icing my knees. Freestylers, backstrokers, and butterflyers usually have shoulder problems, but most breaststrokers have knee problems, advised to ice regularly and take eight aspirin a day. After workouts and races, I would sit in the bleachers with a styrofoam cup of frozen water, rolling the flat ice against the insides of my knees until they turned bright pink and lost all feeling. I'd peel the cup back from the edges so it wouldn't squeak against the numb skin. The ice would become slick, contouring as it melted.

But I don't remember talking to him. I do remember talking to Dawn, the assistant coach, the next morning. Mitch wasn't on deck. We sat in two plastic folding chairs by the side of the pool, watching the team practice. Dawn told me Mitch was angry. She asked me what I was going to do. I think I said take up piano and study art, knowing she wouldn't get it. Knowing maybe even I didn't get it. I remember looking out at the swimmers in the lanes, heading into the hard main set, and thinking: I've crossed the line. I don't have to do that anymore. I remember sitting there and feeling relieved.

Mitch once told me: "You're going to be great." Then Dawn told me: "Mitch doesn't want to talk to you."

When you're a swimmer, coaches stand above you, over you. You look up to them, are vulnerable, naked and wet in front of them. Coaches see you weak, they weaken you, they have your trust, you do what they say. The relationship is guardian, father, mother, boss, mentor, jailer, doctor, shrink, and teacher. My heart broke.

My grandfather was a bomber pilot in the Second World War. Though he lived into his late eighties, he's frozen in my mind as the young man in a photo, wearing a flight suit and goggles, grinning next to a B-25 Mitchell. The image that comes to mind when I think of my mother is a snapshot of her, taken around 1983, sitting on her bed dressed in work clothes: silk shirt, trousers, long necklace, smiling. If I think of my dad, he's in our dining room, clapping and singing along to "The Gambler" by Kenny Rogers. The default image I have of myself is a photo: me, ten, standing next to the ladder at Cawthra Park pool in a blue bathing suit, knees clenched, trying to catch my breath.

I've defined myself, privately and abstractly, by my brief, intense years as an athlete, a swimmer. I practiced five or six hours a day, six days a week, eating and sleeping as much as possible in between. Weekends were spent either training or competing. I wasn't the best; I was relatively fast. I trained, ate, traveled, and showered with the best in the country, but wasn't the best; I was pretty good.

I liked how hard swimming at that level was—that I could do something difficult and unusual. Liked knowing my discipline would be recognized, respected, that I might not be able to say the right things or fit in, but I could do something well. I wanted to believe that I was talented; being fast was proof. Though I loved racing, the idea of fastest, of number one, of the Olympics, didn't motivate me.

I still dream of practice, of races, coaches and blurry competitors. I'm drawn to swimming pools, all swimming pools, no matter how small or murky. When I swim now, I step into the water as though absentmindedly touching a scar. My recreational laps are phantoms of my competitive races.

BYRON

I e-mail one of my old coaches, Byron MacDonald, and ask to sit in on a morning practice at the University of Toronto pool. When I arrive, Byron and his assistant coach, Linda, are standing at the deep end, each holding a photocopy of the workout. They look exactly as I remember them. Byron still has a contained Roy Scheider swagger. Linda's no-bullshit poker face is still quick to laugh.

The pool looks the same too. It has an odd palette for a swimming pool: orange, brown, and beige, with bursts of varsity blue on the pennants, the deck, and the seven letters of TORONTO spaced evenly between each of the eight lanes. When I swam with Byron, I'd wonder what practice was like from on deck, what it felt to be warm and dry up there, in sneakers and shorts. I'd always been curious about the tedium a coach might experience, while the rest of us, in the water, pushed against the thousands of meters of warm-up, main sets, and warm-down. Time passes with precision in a workout, every minute—every second—is felt and accounted for. In other words, time passes slowly.

I'm surprised, then, watching practice from the deck, to find it pass quickly.

I don't glance at the clock for the first forty minutes. Watching Byron's swimmers combing through the water keeps me in a hypnotic focus. Byron stands beside me and describes the trajectory of a few swimmers' careers: one is the team's best hope for placement on the Canadian Olympic team; another is struggling with an eating disorder; one boy, watching the workout, is sidelined by a broken foot. Between sets Byron announces my presence on the deck, explaining that "Leanne swam with us a couple of years ago." I do a quick calculation in my head. It's been exactly twenty years, to the month.

Byron has replaced the analog pace clocks, with their four, multicolored sweeping hands, with small, digital ones that perch in the corners of the pool. Temporal surveillance cameras. He still says things like "Let's go on the top" or "Everyone in the water on the top," referring to the red hand of the clock reaching the number 60 at the top of the face. His expressions jolt me back into the firm macro-grip on time I had as swimmer. The ability to make still lifes out of tenths of seconds.

As we watch the team, Byron directs my attention to one swimmer, a boy whose turns are remarkable. Linda corrects a girl's backstroke, explaining that she needs to lead with her shoulder not her hand, and I remember being the recipient of that kind of attention, knowing there was perfection to trace and retrace, unwavering details of technical precision that, on good days, made practice a sharpening, rather than the unraveling it usually felt like to me. I loved drills best, when I could feel the water in centimeters and so understand how tiny adjustments and angles added up and propelled my body more efficiently. We'd move slowly up and down the pool, sculling with only our hands and wrists, or swim backstroke pointing to the ceiling with one hand and pausing for the other hand to catch up. I liked the idea of bodies as hydrodynamic, the eddies and ripples, the repetition, the needlepoints of swimming.

Byron takes me through the changes the sport has undergone in the past twenty years. He illustrates each detail—technical suits, track blocks, false-start rules—with trivia-studded anecdotes. He furnishes last names and years, recounts heartbreaking stories of disqualifications and losses, adds gossip, footnotes inventions and media coverage with a born storyteller's delivery. I ask him if anyone's ever made a pun on his name and that of Lord Byron, the water-loving poet and swimmer of the Hellespont. He laughs and says no, that maybe the only appropriate time to have done it was when he competed for Canada at the Munich Olympics in 1972.

SWIMMING STUDIES

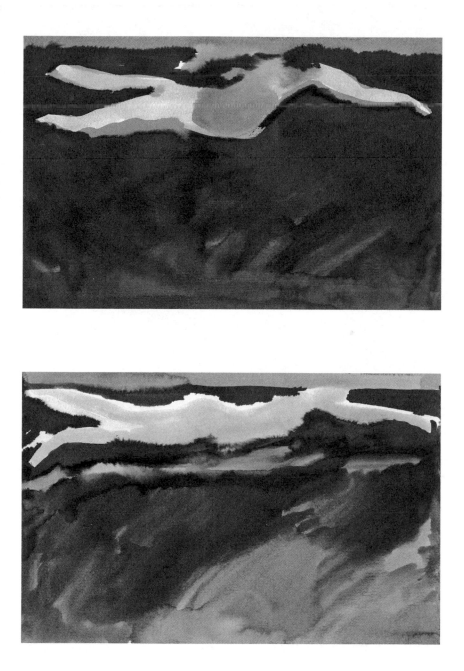

FINALS

On a wet November afternoon, I drive my rented Ford Focus to the Etobicoke Olympium to watch the finals of a national swim meet.

The easiest way to describe the insular, clammy, circumscribed, and largely underexposed world of competitive swimming is to explain what finals are like.

I sit with Linda and Byron, high in the wooden bleachers. The waffled rows of seating look as they did twenty years ago: a mess, like the open drawers of a giant chest, sloppy with duffel bags, candy-colored towels, damp swimmers, perspiring coaches, heat sheets, papers, and clothes. And food. Two swimmers eat raw vegetables from a cardboard box of produce. A coach peels an orange. A girl crams gorp into her mouth while a boy unwraps a foil package, cuts a section of chocolate-chip banana bread with a plastic knife, and chews it thoughtfully. The benches are strewn with granola bar wrappers and empty water bottles. Another boy drinks a fresh muddy-brown protein shake, the mini-blender blades dripping onto his feet. Bright blue and green sports drinks are stuffed into sneakers atop algebra textbooks, iPads and iPods, and T-shirts. *Talking* T-shirts. They have the testosterone tone of action-movie trailers, amped up and motivational. Directly in front of me, the backs of three swimmers advise me to *SEE THE INVISIBLE / FEEL THE INTANGIBLE / ACHIEVE THE IMPOSSIBLE; RISE TO THE CHALLENGE; IN ORDER TO IMPROVE, ATTEMPT THE IMPOSSIBLE.* Farther down the bleachers, a fourth reassures me that *A CHAMPION NEVER STANDS ON THE PODIUM ALONE.*

It is a long-course (LC) meet, which means the races are swum in fifty meters rather than twenty-five, the length of most Canadian community pools. Competitions held in twenty-five-meter or twenty-five-yard pools are referred to as short-course (SC).

The swimming calendar has two seasons. The SC, from September to March, and the LC, from April to August. Both seasons culminate in national-level meets like this one, open to all ages, with morning preliminary heats and evening finals. Minimum qualifying times are posted by Swimming Canada, the national governing body of competitive swimming. These are usually the thirty-sixth-place time in each event from the previous year's national championship.

Because of these time standards—provincial, national, and international—swimmers' goals are temporal and their efforts interior rather than adversarial or gladiatorial. The sport is judged by the indifferent clock.

When I swam, I always saw familiar faces in my heats, but I knew them by their times—in descending tenths and hundredths of seconds—as much as by their names.

This is what a pool, outfitted for a big meet, looks like:

At either end of each of the eight lanes of a long-course pool is a starting block. (Some Olympic-standard pools have ten lanes, but the races use only the middle eight of those ten.) All races over fifty meters start from the same end. The blocks are fitted with an angled back panel where a swimmer can rest one foot higher than the other, for extra traction during the start.

Each block holds an individual speaker that transmits the sound of the starting horn evenly. The blocks are also fitted with a light that flashes when the horn sounds, for the hearing-impaired. (Since light moves faster than sound, some swimmers choose to react to the light.)

Wired to the block are two timing plungers, coiled cords synched with the starting horn, used as backup if the swimmer has a soft finish (not exerting enough pressure at the wall to register a time) or if the touchpads fail. These are started electronically and stopped manually by two of three officials who are stationed behind each block. The third official times the race manually with a stopwatch.

The officials, required to dress in head-to-toe white, are volunteers. They are parents of swimmers, parents of former swimmers, or former swimmers themselves. During races, the area around and behind each block is understood to be a place of private focus—an invisible box thick with tension. Even though the timers and officials share it, the swimmers ignore them or treat them with minimal politesse.

In the pool, affixed to the wall at the ends of each lane are wide yellow panels, bisected vertically by a black stripe. These are pressure-sensitive touchpads, used to make the most accurate record of a swimmer's finish. The lanes are demarcated by lane ropes: buoyant plastic discs, strung together along a taut wire. The three middle lane ropes, marking lanes four and five, are strung with yellow discs. This is to indicate where the two fastest qualifiers swim—a practice developed to help television audiences recognize those lanes. Lane ropes are always a solid color five meters from either end, and at fifteen meters from each wall are marked in red. Swimmers must surface after turns and starts before or at the mark, or they will be disqualified. A thin rope is strung across the width of the pool to further judge this rule. Also strung across the pool, five meters from each end, are backstroke flags. These festive plastic triangles (which remind me of used-car lots) are used by backstrokers to gauge turns and finishes. Near the competition pool, there is usually a warm-down pool, often the diving tank, where swimmers do relaxed laps after races in order to keep lactic acid from building up.

After the Canadian national anthem is played and the bagpipe-led officials are paraded onto deck, the consolation, or B, final of the women's 100m breaststroke is swum. These women had the ninth through sixteenth fastest times from heats. As they climb out of the water, eight more women are introduced. This is the A final, the first through eighth fastest qualifiers. The women are marched along the deck to thumping pop music, in this case "Raise Your Glass" by Pink. They all wear caps and goggles, and some, a second cap over their goggle straps. Their team logo is printed on both sides, and on occasion, the swimmer's last name. They wear baggy variations on tracksuits, parkas, and team uniforms; towels slung over their shoulders, hoods up, earbuds inserted. Their feet are shod in sneakers, deck sandals, flip-flops, or UGGs, or are bare. Behind the blocks, the women jump up and down, pointing their toes. They stretch their legs over the blocks, compulsively adjust and readjust their caps and goggles, pummel their thighs with fists, fling arms back and across, back and across their bodies, suckle water bottles, adjust their blocks, and pull on the straps of their tight competition suits. They are twitching, readying.

The woman with the fastest time after preliminary heats occupies lane four. Second-fastest is in lane five, third in lane three. The rest, in descending order, are in lanes six, two, seven, one, and finally, eight. This placement accounts for the inverted-V formation that typically occurs during a race. A swimmer who leads from lane one, two, seven, or eight is often called "outside smoke."

The meet official announces each swimmer's name, beginning with lane one. The referee will indicate, with a few short blasts of a whistle, that the swimmers must remove their shoes and clothing. At this point the swimmers stretch, rotate their arms, waggle their heads, bend to the pool and splash water onto themselves. Some stand still, hands on hips. A long whistle indicates that the swimmers are to approach and step onto the starting blocks. The crowd settles into silence. Over the microphone the starter intones, "Take your mark—" and the swimmers bend and freeze with at least one foot touching the front of the block.

Here is a composite sketch of each tensed figure: In lane one is an eighteen-year-old vegetarian who keeps spiders as pets. Her mother died of cancer when she was twelve. Lane two, age seventeen, suffers from severe allergies and chronic eczema but is wary of using antihistamines and topical steroids because of random drug testing. It is lane three's nineteenth birthday, but her boyfriend, who goes to university in Alberta, has not remembered. Her little brother's best friend—who developed a crush on her after she pointed at a houseplant and said, "What is this? Corn?"—wished her a happy birthday as she walked by him on the way to the ladies' locker room, but she did not hear him. Lane four, age seventeen, knows that a coach from the University of Michigan is in the stands hoping to recruit her, and can't stop her hands from shaking. Lane five, nineteen, has been yawning. This is alarming because it usually means she will have a bad race. Lane six, also nineteen, chose a Snickers over a PowerBar half an hour before the race, and some caramel is stuck in an upper left molar. She was worrying it with her tongue during the march but has since forgotten it in a tunnel of concentration. She silently repeats *Okay, okay, okay* to herself. Lane seven's parents are going through a divorce. Last weekend when her father came to pick up her two little brothers, he brought his new girlfriend, Lorraine.

Her mother went batshit when she saw Lorraine get out of the car, and ran out of the house toward her, screaming obscenities and then yanking down Lorraine's yellow strapless top. Her father kept saying calmly, "Lorr, get back in the car." Lane seven watched all of this unfold from her bedroom window. She is fifteen. Lane eight visualizes a white blankness; she hears deck noise as if through a cloud of cotton balls, having tried the sequence of meditation exercises her stepfather taught her, just before the race. She is not speaking to her teammate in lane four, since lane four made out with her ex-boyfriend at a party two weekends ago. She is seventeen.

When the swimmers are perfectly still, the starter's horn makes a loud *bleep*. In unison, the swimmers launch themselves over the water into something that resembles a tiny midair push-up, followed by a small flex at their hips, and enter the water. Lane five, the yawner, has the best start, hitting the water just ahead of the field. In the mid-1990s, the Fédération Internationale de Natation (or FINA, the international governing body of swimming) established a zero-tolerance false-start rule. If someone in the race starts before the gun, the race proceeds and the disqualification occurs at the finish, announced over the loudspeaker.

The race, two lengths of the fifty-meter pool, is considered a sprint. Lane five leads, but at the fifty-meter mark—the split—she is outtouched by lane three. Lane three has a strong turn, with a powerful kick.

Here is what it sounds like to lane three at the wall: A low thump as her hands hit the touchpad. Brief cheering at an intake of breath, collapsing into bubbles as her head, aligned and steady, dips back and under again at the turn. This is followed immediately by quiet. There is a rippling during the long stroke of her underwater pullout, a tight, thin sigh of effort, a gruff exhalation of air, a grunt at the dolphin kick.

As her head breaks the surface, the roar of the crowd is, with each breath, loud then quiet, loud then quiet; a chorus of warbled pops and splashings bursts against the sides of her cap.

The water ahead is smooth and the view is low glassy horizon. Lane four has a grasp of her periphery, but ignores it. Lane five and three are even with her, if not just ahead. Lane four blocks a sinking feeling and starts kicking harder. Between strokes, each swimmer can catch the deep bass of the announcer calling the race over the cheering of the crowd. What they don't hear is that lane eight is creeping up in the last twenty-five meters, and is now even with lane four.

The last ten or fifteen meters are the most painful, physically and mentally. Muscles flood with lactic acid. Strokes shorten, weaken, churn, and find no purchase. It's a terrible, desperate feeling, where the results of training are determined.

Not enough cardio and your entire body fails, not enough drills and your stroke slips, not enough strength training and muscles burn like paper curling in flames.

Lane three touches first, followed by lane four, just barely outtouching lane eight, in third place by two-hundredths of a second. The swimmers turn, heaving, to look at the big scoreboard that displays each lane's time. When lane eight sees her third-place finish she smashes her palm into the yellow wall. Lane five is fourth, followed by six, seven, two, and one.

Lane three pulls off her cap and tosses it onto the deck, then dips her head back to feel the cool water on her head. A whistle is blown. The swimmers haul themselves out of the pool, gather their towels and clothes. Some head for the warm-down pool, others to their coaches.

During the medal ceremony, a woman in a tight black cocktail dress and red heels hands each swimmer a cellophane-wrapped rose, places a medal over her wet head, shakes her right hand. Then each medalist turns to the other two. Lane four hesitates before offering her hand to lane eight. Lane eight shakes it, then, stepping off the podium, wipes her palm on her thigh.

DOUGHNUTS

I join the Town of Mississauga Aquatic Club (TOMAC) swim team with my brother, Derek. He is fourteen, I am twelve. Within the club, our group—Intermediate Age Group—is for the slowest members; the beginners mixed in with the arguably untalented, regardless of age. We are also the least disciplined, required to attend only five practices a week. Advanced Age Groupers have to make eleven. Advanced Age Group is the next level up, where the serious, the crème de la crème of the fifteen-and-unders, swim. Senior level is next, the fastest swimmers fifteen and over. A handful of swimmers from these two groups usually place well at national meets, ranking in the top twenty-five nationally.

Our coach, Tom, is the most fun. He is big and rangy, with a thick dark mustache and a hound-dog face. He drives a red Toyota hatchback with a grubby lamb's-wool steering-wheel cover. At practice, he shuffles up and down the puddled pool deck yelling encouragement and eyeballing our lopsided strokes. He wears deck sandals with gray wool socks, soggy half an hour in.

In winter, when the humidity inside the pool building gets too high and the air we're breathing too hot, Tom opens the double steel doors that lead to the parking lot. A rectangular cloud of steam piles five feet above the water's surface. The cooler air is thick with chlorine, and when I look at the overhead lights through my goggles, they have lemon-yellow halos. The end of the lane is visible only underwater.

After Saturday practice, Tom stations himself, a paper cup of vending machine coffee, and a box of forty Timbits, Tim Hortons doughnut holes, on the benches outside the locker rooms. The Timbits are always all one kind, usually sugar-glazed or glazed chocolate. This fascinates me. I accept that having as many different flavors as possible is better—I demo-cratically believe in assorted. But seeing such a concentration of one good flavor of doughnut hole looks more like abun-dance. Tom may also have known that with assorted there were always orphan duds left rolling in the bottom of the box.

As we wait for our parents, we take one or two Timbits and joke around with Tom. The three older boys who drive to practice ignore the doughnuts and brush past us, kicking the bars of the doors open, heading out to their cars in the snowy parking lot.

. . .

Within the year, after steady improvement and placing well at meets, I move up to Advanced Age Group to train with coach Greg, which means Derek and I attend separate practices. Once a week, driving home after morning practice, my mother takes me to Country Style and lets me choose a doughnut. I take my time deciding before always choosing the same: a five-cents-more Bavarian cream. My mother orders a coffee and sighs. She sighs a lot. The women behind the counter recognize my mother but rebuff her friendliness. She makes a joke about the cold. She mentions what a nice shade of nail polish a girl is wearing, and says thank you in a funny voice, *Tank you veddy much,* when handed her coffee.

English is not my mother's first language; she is Filipino, and speaks in secretary-pleasant Canadian English, her voice low. She has clear pronunciation except for subtleties in spelling, which mislead her. Those come out wrong. *Thigh food. Eyetalian.* She works Tuesdays and Thursdays as a bookkeeper for a company that manufactures tents, tarpaulins, and outdoor pool covers.

I climb into the backseat with the Bavarian cream, lie on my stomach, and pull the middle seat belt diagonally around myself. We back out of the space. I eat slowly, inspecting the doughnut after every bite.

Some mothers sit in the bleachers during morning workout and watch us plow up and down the pool. Freddy's mother would cheer for him during practices. Mine mixes it up: If it's warm out, she reclines the car seat and naps in the parking lot. Or she'll drive back home for more sleep, setting the alarm for six-fifty. Sometimes she'll kill time drinking coffee in the doughnut shop with other mothers, occasionally a father.

I don't like it when my mother watches me practice, and at a certain point I tell my parents I prefer if they don't watch me race. This has something to do with being looked at, seen—I'm self-conscious about my body—and with staking my own territory. They respect this and back off a bit; my mother drops me off and picks me up at practice, drops me off and picks me up at heats and finals.

My father stands in the living room picture window as we back out of the driveway in the car on our way to finals. He raises his hand in a "V for Victory" sign and grins. I watch him until he disappears past the maple tree. As I rest my feet on the dash, I wonder what he'll do next. Maybe he'll watch the car until it is out of sight behind the maple tree, then go back to his studio and the snowbrush he is designing.

My father works in a glassed-in room at the back of our house, on a large, pale green, Borco-covered drafting table. The surface is stacked with onionskin paper, straightedges, and T-squares that remind me of crucifixes. We are not allowed to touch the color-coded carousel of markers that stands in one corner of the table. Derek asks my father why they stink. "Benzene," he replies.

One night, I may have been seven, I watched him work at his table, hooking my fingers, eye level, into the pencil tray. Laid out in a circle of lamplight were heavy red paper, our black-handled kitchen scissors, and four sharp blue-and-black Staedtler drafting pencils. He began drawing letters on the red paper.

"What's that?"

"It's for your mom."

The scissors made a low sound, sure and careful. He was cutting out words. He made a final snip and held up his work like a string of paper dolls.

HAPPY ANNIVERSARY HON

It was the first time I'd seen the word "Hon." It had been just a soft, blurry burr in our house; I had no idea that it was spelled H-O-N, or that it stood for "Honey." The sound of it between my parents gave a sense of calm. Here, though, in tomato-red paper, was a Gothic "HON" for my mother. My father pasted it into a cream-colored card and handed it to me to inspect. I flipped it open and closed a few times.

"It's good."

"Thanks."

He smiled, I handed it back.

In the middle of practice, mind numb with the endless counting of lengths, arms and legs bored with strain, sick of Greg's voice, frustrated by my slow times and the punishing pace, I imagine what my mother might be doing:

She pulls into the Country Style at the corner of the Queensway and Dixie Road to buy a coffee. She orders it to go, but takes a seat, still in her coat, at one of the tables by the dark window. She sits silently, tired, taking small sips. Sometimes her lips move, as she talks a little to herself. Sometimes she shakes her head and raises her eyebrows. At five forty-five she leaves, still holding her cup. She pushes past the two sets of doors, walks to the station wagon, and gets in. She fixes the cup of coffee in the dashboard cup holder, pulls the seat belt across her lap, and turns on the headlights. Inside the doughnut shop the women behind the counter glance up at her inching out of her space, then go back to doing other things.

My thoughts are interrupted by a floater: Pale. Opaque. A perfectly detailed chunk of phlegm, suspended a foot below the surface. It looms in my path like something from *Jaws 3-D*. Seeing it makes me gag, and I wave at it, trying to push it into another lane.

I remember the moment I knew I was not going to go to the Olympics: I am fourteen, it is five-thirty a.m., a quarter of the way into practice. I'm swimming sloppily, staring hard at the stripe on the bottom of the pool. Though we're still warming up, I'm exhausted. My arms hurt, legs hurt, lungs hurt, and I think, grimly: What for? I'm fed up with the steady pain, the mechanical cycle of breathe-pull-pull-breathe-pull-pull, and the dull gray noise of churning water. Then it comes to me, gently, in a quiet flash: I am not going to go to the Olympics. I will not be going. Not me. I fight off the thought, crumpling it in my head as negative and defeatist. I finish practice, sluggishly shower, change, and wait at the community center entrance for my mother to pick me up. When I get in the car—sullen, damp, and oblivious to her fatigue—I complain that she is late. We drive in silence. As we approach Country Style, she turns into the drive and parks. My wet hair is frozen to the window where I've leaned on it.

I still have, from that following spring of 1988, a navy blue T-shirt that reads, in fading white letters, *TOMAC '88 Olympic Trials Team*. The 1988 Canadian Olympic swimming trials were split over two meets: one in May in Montreal, and the other in August in Etobicoke, where swimmers had a second chance to fill the team spots that hadn't been filled in May. The blue T-shirt could have been from either. Trying to recall the meets, I draw a blank. I remember being in Montreal, but it's all dark vignettes: waiting in the Piscine Olympique lobby near some vending machines; the big bright ladies' locker rooms, orange and yellow, rows of bathing suits hung drying from locker padlocks; a gleaming room of column showers. I'd turned fifteen by the August trials, yet all that remain are my times in *Swim Magazine* and a three-minute videotape of one of my two consolation finals. I was third in that race, eleventh overall.

It's as though these two meets have—like what I had for lunch two days ago—been totally forgotten. Like something I said that impressed someone but don't remember saying. I nod, right, sure, wondering if they're mistaken. Wonder how it's possible that I can remember a booger more vividly than any details from my first Olympic trials.

SWEATSHIRTS

Departure is from the Square One shopping mall parking lot, early Friday morning. My mother pulls up alongside the bright bus that churns plumes of exhaust into the frozen air. After checking that I have my money belt (tightly Velcroed between my track pants and underwear) and slipping me an extra twenty-dollar bill, she kisses me good-bye. I shove my suitcase into the gaping side of the bus, shoulder my team duffel, wave, and board. I get two seats to myself. After a roll call, the bus cloverleafs onto the highway and I make a bed of my parka and pillow. For the first hour, the bus cabin is filled with loud giggling, girly mewling, and ass-slapping playfights. Long limbs spill over the arms and backs of seats as our bodies try to get comfortable. Sweatshirts are loud with fading varsity logos: *Russell Athletics! Champion! Roots Sports! Speedo! Arena Pro!* *"TOMAC"* is stamped in navy blue and kelly green on bags, T-shirts, and sweatshirts. I'm wearing my Christmas present, a thick *Beaver Canoe* sweatshirt, stiff from the wash. I feel safe in it, that I look like something recognizable.

I am thirteen years old and sweatshirts are my metric, sweatshirts mean everything. They stand for who and how I want to be. I believe in their prep school palette of inclusion blue, privileged pink, the felted lettering, crests, membership, belonging. I am small but slouch around in L or XL.

Hour two. Along the ceiling of the bus the lights switch off one by one. Eyes close and mouths fall open. Elbows and knees flop. There is a sweet and sleepy whiff of recently un-laundered pillowcase. The sounds of the bus are lulling: engine humming evenly, steady breathing, the scraping of textbook pages turned, the tinny smashing of Sony Walkmans, volume cranked.

We pull into the parking lot of a twenty-four-hour restaurant. The overhead lights come on and swimmers stir. Some reach groggily for their bags and wallets, mumbling all at once:

"You want anythi—"

"Can I borrow a few dollars?"

"Where are—"

"God, what's that smell?"

"You smell—"

"Where's my—"

"Grab me a hash brown?"

A Senior boy makes his way down the aisle, slapping each headrest hard as he goes by, bleary annoyance in his wake. The girls brush their brassy hair back with their hands, pull it into elastics, stuff hands into mittens. Cheeks and lips are rosy with sleep and wear the inward, glum glaze of athletes at rest.

A few of my teammates leap the bus steps and bounce up and down in the icy air, pull their hands inside their cuffs, and lope toward the restaurant. I remain on the bus and watch them, my head pressed close to the cold window. They hunch against the wind and yank their coats around themselves. I can tell who they are by their bodies and gaits, but their first names are embroidered on the shoulders of their identical parkas: *Brad, Karen, Andrew, Stephanie.* One swimmer, Duncan, has a big sheepskin coat instead of a parka. It was his father's, and it's coming apart at the armpits.

Leaning back, I look at my reflection, sharp in the dark window, then at the yellow restaurant sign, then back at my reflection. I look like a boy; my hair is dry and puffy, eyes slightly too close together. By my watch we've been on the road for two and a half hours. Halfway.

I climb out of my seat to get my bag from the overhead compartment. In the end pocket are six Oh Henry! chocolate bars. I take one, settle in, and eat it, studying the fabric pattern on the back of the seat in front of me. My eyes are locked in a zombie stare. I think vaguely about the squiggles and specks as I chew.

My mother bought the chocolate bars from Hy & Zel's pharmacy in the Dixie Value Mall. There are wire bins of them—alongside bins of shampoo, pink razors, and licorice, everything three for ninety-nine cents—at the entrance of the store. I see a different side of my mother at Dixie Value Mall. There's a laser focus in her browsing, a discerning gaze I never see her use anywhere else. She loves nice clothes and has an eye for fashion. We have pictures of her from the early 1960s, modeling white asymmetrical gowns in the Philippines.

She buys magazines from time to time, *Vogue* and *Elle*, close-ups of beautiful women with glossy fuchsia lips and shiny bangs on the covers. (Her only subscription, though, is to *Chatelaine*, a Canadian women's magazine that seems more about salads and what to put on cuts and scrapes.) In the car once, she told me that she used to wish her nose were pointier, whiter, less wide, and that as a girl she went to bed with it pinched in a clothespin. My father always tells me that her nose was one of the things he noticed first about her, that he loves it.

In stores, when my mother holds a top or a dress to her body and looks in the mirror, she juts her jaw a little and glares half lidded at her reflection. I hate that face, but my own seduction by clothing follows hers—the version of myself that I yearn for squints back at me when I pose before a mirror.

I have specific ideas about my thirteen-year-old wardrobe, informed by sitcoms, music videos, and illustrations on the covers of young adult paperbacks. I insist on minute details: sweatpants have to be gray, the cotton has to be a certain grade and thickness, shoes have to fit over the instep so that the laces are evenly spaced. Under a red sweater I could wear only a white shirt. White turtlenecks look best under V-necks, and pants should make your bum a triangle. When I follow a trend (plastic bracelets, neon Lycra), I get nervous. Mosquitoes and wasps are attracted to my fluorescent-yellow sweatshirt. I spend an unhappy year in seventh grade trying to look preppy with the wrong ingredients (cheap cotton shirts, the colors too heavy and bright; fake-leather penny loafers; acrylic cable-knit sweaters). Photographs from that time show a boyish girl, sad and stiff.

My father protests when my mother buys herself new clothes. Doesn't she understand they just can't afford it? They can't afford it. They just cannot afford it. Her silence hangs in the house like the smell of burnt toast.

One night, my husband, James, comes to bed in a pair of blue oxford boxer shorts, with a T-shirt that I found in a pile of things a coworker was giving away. The shorts have a little polo horse embroidered on one leg. I recognize the horse and its simple threaded colors. It's the horse from the shirts that teammates and classmates wore in sixth, seventh, and eighth grades. Shirts my best friend and her brothers wore, stained, lost.

"You have no idea how much that little horse thing meant to me," I tell James, tracing the threads on his cuff, "how many hours and weeks and months I spent thinking about that horse, wanting it, wishing I could have that horse."

"Really?"

I tell James that my parents disapproved of spending more than ten dollars on an item of clothing. How, in 1986, something that cost forty dollars was disgraceful. How I saved and saved my paper-route cash, my dollar-a-day allowance, earned by emptying and loading the dishwasher, vacuuming the stairs. How one Friday night I slept over at my best friend Danielle's. Her mother dropped us off at Yorkdale Mall on Saturday, and

I took an hour choosing a plaid cotton shirt, boys' size 18. How I still have the shirt, never being able to give it up. How baffled my parents were at my first act of rebellion.

"Want to see it?"

I go to the closet and come back with the shirt, droopy on a hanger. It's a pastel cacophony. Every color in the world seems to be gridded into the thin cotton: a weird, postcolonial mess of madras.

"This is Polo?" James is suspicious. "This isn't Ralph Lauren."

A small swell of panic. Then I locate the horse. "Look."

The pale blue embroidered horse is barely visible against a pale blue, green, and mauve field.

"You can't even see it!" James laughs. "It's so *you* to have picked out the one shirt where you couldn't even see it!"

I stroke the smooth threads of the tiny horse and tell James that when I bought it, I thought it was the nicest one in the cubbyhole of shirts, I thought the colors would go with everything. That though I was dismayed at the imperceptible horse, I bought it anyway and figured I could make do. That I used to take a blue pen and color the horse in darker when I wore it.

"Look at the colors. Preppy vomit. So not me."

I put the shirt on; it still fits.

James tilts his head. "Well, it doesn't *not* suit you. . . ."

. . .

My teammates return and push down the aisle, carrying takeaway cups and paper bags, trailing cold parking-lot air. The food perfumes the bus. Mary S. offers me a corner of hash brown. After a head count, the bus sighs and pulls out of the parking lot. I turn around, lay my temple on the armrest, and watch the overhead reading lights come on. I hear the unzipping of parkas and loud drawn-out burping. From my sideways view I see running shoes being slipped off and feet in white athletic socks poking into the aisle, soft and curving like hockey sticks.

I turn onto my back and look out my window. It frames a stoic northern landscape: the snow glows blue against long, dark whale-like swells of Precambrian Canadian shield. The tall pines, silhouetted against the navy sky, are a deep, living black, treetops rushing up and down like a giant electrocardiogram.

I wake as the bus pulls into a hotel parking lot and stops. I look out my window: a thin gray morning. The driver pulls on his parka, wraps a scarf twice around his head, and exits. He opens the side of the bus, and begins to stack luggage on the pavement. It's mostly team duffel bags. Clipped to them are kickboards and foam pull buoys with surnames hand-printed in permanent marker: *Fedoruk, Chase, Creelman, Lang.* A few pieces look like honeymoon suitcases. Sky-blue plastic, Black Watch tartan, some pale tan with big gold buckles and stickers from Cancún. I watch the driver set down my father's small black suitcase, with the broken front-pocket zipper.

In our room, Andrea drops her bags on the floor and dramatically falls facedown on a bed in her parka and boots. I unpack, brush my teeth, and put on my pajamas. Mary L. kicks off her shoes and curls under the covers in her parka, then immediately springs back up and unpacks her food. She places a jar of peanut butter, a box of crispy-chewy chocolate chip cookies, a bunch of bananas, and five granola bars on the desk. She twists open a jar of blueberry baby food and eats it with her index finger. I pull the heavy drapes closed and get into bed. We have two hours before heats.

LAUNDRY

London, 2010. At eight a.m. I set out from the house, toward the Hampstead Heath Ladies' Pond. I can see my breath as I wend my way up the overgrown front path; I exhale long and slow to watch it as I cross the road and walk past a couple of magpies. *One for sorrow, two for joy.* On my right, the Long Pond is dark and green, then, over a hill and around a bend, the Mixed Pond grayish-brown on my left. I can feel the cold air through my sweater. September.

Three people are unfolding tables near a van in preparation for a marathon. In a wooded path two joggers pass, smelling of shampoo and laundry, lemony. The path dips and I hear women's laughter, its pitch distinctive. Voices carry crisp and dense over water, heads held high and tipped back to speak. The effort makes for breathy, cheerful barking. I can't see the Ladies' Pond, but I can hear it.

The pond water temperature, neatly written on a blackboard, is fourteen degrees Celsius. Two women circle the life preservers at the far end. Another swims steadily out toward a lily-padded patch. Two more stroke toward the concrete dock, one in a yellow cap. A few ducks and a pair of swans bob in the corner.

I know I have to get in without hesitating, one smooth movement from the top of the ladder into the murk. I slip in until my shoulders are submerged—the water stings and my breath balls in my throat, high and shallow. I can see only a few inches of my body before it dissolves into the olive dark.

I swim, moving every limb exaggeratedly to generate heat, then push facedown to the farthest life preserver, toward the two women. When I get there I raise my head. One woman talks about how her child is adjusting to school. The other makes noises of assent and sympathy. I wonder: Did they come here as friends or befriend each other in the pond? How long have they been swimming in water this cold? Will I ever have a friend who swims in freezing ponds with me? I circle again and my body feels warm, but it is the warmth of a slap: blood rushing the flesh. Looking back toward the dock, I see another woman, wearing a black tank and a white cap, step calmly down the ladder.

After another turn I get out and wrap myself in the fluffy gray bath towel I grabbed from the bathroom of the house where I'm renting a room. My breath is still tight in my chest. The towel smells lemony too.

The unnaturally sweet laundry smell is a match scraped against deep feelings of longing. I'm obsessed with this smell. A detergent-fragrant scarf bought on eBay arrives in the mail and I debate whether to write the seller and ask what brand she washed it in. I buy unscented soap for my dermatitic skin, can't quite bring myself to buy dryer sheets, but part of me still wants my life to be suburb-scented.

When I was little, our family laundry was done with no-name detergent and line-dried until well into November. It didn't smell like anything to me. Now when I visit my parents' home and press my face into a towel, I smell my family. My mother's Filipino homemaking and my father's citrus-scrub mechanic's hand cleaner. The smell is mildly tarpaulin, with notes of canvas, bamboo, and limonene. Comforting, but harsh.

Edmonton, Alberta, 1987. I wake in the middle of the night, and by the color of the darkness and the sound of an aquarium I know I'm not at home. I blink, lie very still, and remember: Jen, Stephanie, and I are being billeted in the basement of somebody's Edmonton home. I am lying on my side on a pullout couch; my two sleeping teammates are in the room, Jen on a couch across from me, Stephanie on a mattress on the floor.

It is warm in my Miss Piggy sleeping bag—we are all in sleeping bags—and smells like the inside of a van. My mother made a liner, two striped twin bedsheets sewn together, and I'm twisted inside them, beneath Miss Piggy's giant lashed eyes, her mouth slightly open in a happy Muppety expression. The clock on my new yellow stopwatch, wound around my wrist, reads 4:15 a.m.

I close my eyes and try to sleep again, but I'm thinking of hotel rooms, the comforting sterile non-smell, the hum of ice machines. I'm thinking of breakfast upstairs in the kitchen of this house in a few hours, of demonstrating table manners, the strange swimmers from the other team whose house this is, their non-swimming siblings, cheerful chatter, and the selection of breakfast cereal. I always wind up eating too much or too little in other people's houses. I hope the billeting mother will not make eggs.

Turning over onto my back I can dimly see a few things on the paneled walls: a poster of Corey Hart, another of a baseball team, a framed landscape. I close my eyes. The meet starts tomorrow. We drove straight to the Edmonton pool from the airport, lugging our bags through the locker rooms and onto the deck. It was an easy practice. I used a yellow kickboard that belonged to a swimmer from the University of Calgary team, the Dinos, and I wanted to steal it.

I decide to do my race. I turn onto my stomach, tuck my head into the sleeping bag and begin. My stopwatch beeps and wakes Stephanie.

"What the—?"

Before every race I'd rub my hands on the top of the block to make them raw and more sensitive in the water. I'd know the push, the ripping sound of entry, the silence, the gauging of depth, and the repetitive, urging noises when my head broke the surface of the water. I could always recognize my coach's voice in the crowd. (The images, the intense anticipation and strain I'd conjure in bed, would be replaced, a decade later, with the men I'd imagine sleeping with.)

As I touch and turn for the last length, hackneyed expressions like *pour it on, flat out, mad dash, closing in* spool in my head. Suddenly the yellow Omega touchpad. I click down hard on my stopwatch: the blue digits read 1:12:07.

The sound of the aquarium.

"Fucking enough with the beeping and panting already. It's like four in the morning."

Stephanie, from the mattress on the floor.

. . .

I stand for a few chilly minutes and watch the pond. Two women get out, another gets in. I gather my things. In the shedlike locker room I watch what the other women do, and imitate them. They strip down and rinse the pond water from their suits and bodies. Standing under a lukewarm shower I eavesdrop. One woman swears by her partial wetsuit, another swims through to December. Something about a school, about a woman they all know, about someone else's handbag. We face the walls as we change, our skin white and red. As I head back across the heath I wave to the guards, the damp towel wrapped double around my neck and over my nose so I can walk along breathing in its smell, now mixed with a greenish whiff of duckweed.

.

FOURTEEN ODORS

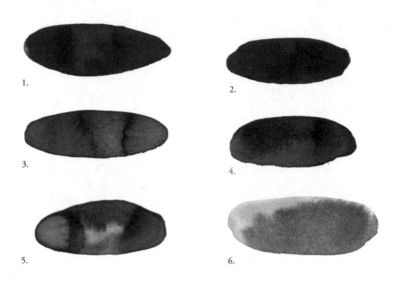

1. Clarkson High School parking lot, 4:52 a.m.: Wet brick, notes of rubber, gasoline, and cigarettes.

2. Teammate's hair: Finesse conditioner circa 1987, released when hair is pulled out, damp, from a tight ponytail.

3. Mother's breath: Coffee, warm skin, seat belt, wet acrylic mitten, resignation, Nivea Creme undertone.

4. Duffel bag pocket: Tangy nylon, porcini. Hint of oats and semisweet chocolate chip.

5. Wrist beneath watch strap: Vaseline Intensive Care, iodine, and banana.

6. Parka hem: Apple core, halogen, polyester shearling, dried ketchup.

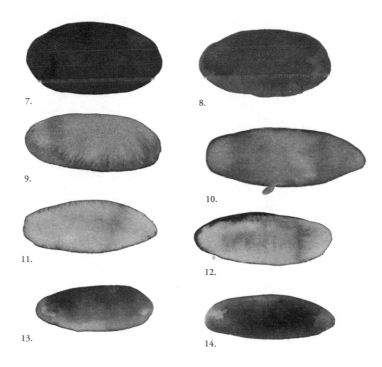

7. Sit-ups partner: Tide, milk, terrier, and grape Hubba Bubba.

8. Wet team towel: Heavy notes of chlorine, light notes of garlic, lakeside dock, and brown bread.

9. Ladies' locker room toilet stall: Bleach, baby powder, mild urine, and faint ammonia.

10. Coach: Fresh laundry, windbreaker nylon, Mennen Speed Stick, Magic Marker, and bologna.

11. Pillow: Chlorine, mildew, faint clove and starchy mucus scent.

12. Male teammate: Blue cheese, Polo cologne, suntan lotion, fenugreek.

13. Fingernail: Chlorine, barbecue potato chip, wool mitten.

14. Silver medal: Petroleum, nylon, mineral water, and strawberry.

CROWN ASSETS

I can't find a swimsuit in Toronto the day before my wedding reception. All the stores stock in mid-February are skirted, boob-padded backless styles in tropical patterns. At Lululemon, I find a two-piece outfit designed for Bikram yoga.

"It's designed to get wet," the salesclerk explains, "but it hasn't been tested in chlorine, so it might lose its color."

It's black. I take it.

The hotel swimming pool is fifteen meters long. On one side is an unlit fireplace, on the other a blue-tiled shower and a few chairs and tables spread with Canadian fashion magazines.

The water is bath temperature. I swim a few laps, then decide to do a hundred. This is my default workout, one hundred reps of whatever. One hundred is actually not much, but it sounds nice, like "an hour," even though swimming a hundred laps of this short a pool does not take an hour, it takes about twenty minutes. At each end I count a number to myself. If I lose count, I round down to the last number remembered. As I swim, my mind wanders. I talk to myself. What I can see through my goggles is boring and foggy, the same view lap by lap. Mundane, unrelated memories flash up vividly and randomly, a slide show of shuffling thoughts. They flash up and fade, like the thoughts that float peripherally before sleep, either inconsequential or gathering momentum into anxiety before eventually dissolving. Each thought lasts a quarter-lap or half-lap, a couple of laps tops. My responses to these thoughts are burbled into the water at my lips, improvements on history—things I wish I'd said or been able to say: "No, I'd rather not watch your bag." *"Oui, en taille trente-six, s'il vous plaît."* "Your spouse is not invited."

Lap 15, My dog: I walked my dog half of the two miles to the deli before remembering it closed at five p.m. on Sundays. We turned back and passed a woman getting into her car, who gave me a small smile. She put a bundle of paper bags into her trunk, which appeared to be stuffed with quilts.

. . .

Lap 22, Annette: That time we went for a walk. As we were passing the graveyard she explained why she doesn't bother to send us thank-you notes anymore, and I noticed a figure clad in camouflage walking behind us at a faster pace.

Lap 31, Dad: He wore a black-and-orange-striped full-body snowsuit. On his head was a brown and orange balaclava, its eye and mouth openings folded up over his forehead. I know the smell of the inside of the hat, remember wearing it and scaring myself in the mirror. As we walked our road, my dad talked about his health and the health of his dog.

Lap 35, Donkey costume: Laura and I decide to surprise James with his present: a donkey costume. Laura will approach the house from the woods wearing it, and I instruct Bruce to coax James into position at the window in exactly half an hour. Setting off, Laura holds the papier-mâché donkey head beneath her arm. In the woods she puts the head on, and turns back toward the house. Halfway up the hill Laura gets snared in a patch of hemlock, the needles catching on the furry donkey body.

Lap 40, Derek: My brother prying the top off a can of honey-roasted peanuts, his double-jointed fingers bent almost backward as he does so.

Lap 42, Shopping: The dusty beige-pink color of a pair of trousers I saw in Berlin but did not buy.

Lap 43, Berlin: Jenny in the Holiday Inn swimming pool, grinning widely as she breaststroked up and down. Our flight
• had been canceled and we checked into the suburban hotel after a long day of hearing Delta employees tell us that what we wanted to do was not possible.

The hotel pool has no gutter, so the waves I make are choppy. I glance at the clock from time to time as I switch from freestyle to backstroke, from backstroke to breaststroke, then kick for twenty-five lengths with a small red board.

Lap 45, Sweaters: I like the idea of a V-neck better than the reality.

Lap 49, Conditioner: That time Gus and Jason went to Korea to oversee the printing of Gus's first book of photographs. Jason noticed that Gus's hair was getting greasier and greasier by the day. After four days he brought it up. Gus told him he was baffled too, that he kept using the Korean shampoo and conditioner in the hotel shower. Jason told him the hotel didn't provide conditioner, only hand cream.

Lap 52, Hotels: With a finger, someone has drawn the five Olympic rings on the steamed-up bathroom mirror. Our team occupies ten rooms along a narrow hallway. In most of them, the bathtubs, plastic ice buckets, and sinks are filled with hot water. Thin white hotel towels and thick team towels are spread in front of and between the beds. We strip down to our two-sizes-too-small racing suits and unwrap multipacks of orange, pink, and blue disposable razors. In one room a portable stereo blasts a Simple Minds tape. In my room we play Tears for Fears.

As we shave, the water in the buckets and basins gets cloudy and hairy, the carpets darken, drenched, are flecked with foam, and the rooms and hallways reek of Barbasol and Noxzema. Boys rush into our room with half-beards and half-hawks, strutting between the beds before skip-running down the hall. It is Friday, the first night of the weekend meet. The few swimmers who shaved before heats watch their roommates from the beds, wincing at the inevitable nicks. They offer to shave our backs, hamstrings, and the hard-to-reach parts of our upper arms.

I am rooming with the three Marys. One shaves my back as I lie on my stomach and stare out onto the snowy balcony. We put our cartons of milk and tubs of yogurt just outside the sliding doors to keep cold, and the snow has piled like little hats on top of them. As Mary K. scrapes my shoulder blades and spine, I wonder if the milk will freeze and if my back hair will grow in dark and thick. I do my arms myself.

The meet is a three-day short-course age-group meet, held at Laurentian University in Sudbury, Ontario, Olympian Alex Baumann's hometown. Midwinter, Sudbury is like a lunar station. The ground is white, as are the steaming buildings, bricks, and rooftops. It's a sprawling nickel-mining town, whose spirit feels mineral, scientific and cold.

Later, in bed, after the first night and a spaghetti dinner, the sheets feel cool and smooth against my skin, feel as if I'm slipping through them, as if they're blowing over my body in a breeze that gets gently warmer. I move my legs and arms slowly under the covers in the dark, hoping Mary L., beside me, won't wake up, then roll onto my stomach and press my forehead into my fists. I quietly visualize my 100m breaststroke race with this new, seal-like feeling. I want to swim it in 1:11:00.

When I do this at home, I take a stopwatch to bed, lie on my stomach and put my face in the pillow, tucking my head to make a pocket of air. I press my elbows into my sides, holding the watch in my right hand. Breathing as I do in the race, holding at the turns, I feel slightly light-headed, and a sensation of milky smoothness followed by sudden roughness creeps in at the edges of my perception. Sometimes I get the feeling that my hands are enormous. I near the wall and stop the watch as I hit the yellow touchpad. It reads 1:13:50. Again, 1:14:09. Then 1:09:67.

I usually fall asleep with the stopwatch beside me, but in the morning sometimes find it on my hospital table, its nylon cord wrapped neatly around it. My father brought home two rolling hospital tables one day. They had plastic wood-grain desktops, and bases that rolled under the bed. He found them at Crown Assets, a series of weekend auctions of government-surplus material and seized and lost goods. The house was filled with things from Crown Assets: books, a Shop-Vac, Bombay Company side tables in need of a brass hinge or two. Our army-surplus Dodge van and Plymouth Caravelle (previously an undercover police car) were bought in the auctions. The Caravelle was brown and bulky, but could do over 250 kilometers per hour. The door lock knobs were removed in the back. When my dad locked the doors automatically on family outings, Derek and I would howl and pull on them like captured lunatics.

The hospital table's top panel flips open to reveal a shallow drawer and a small oxidized mirror. I keep my locked diary and some pens and pencil crayons in there. When I tidy my room, I roll the table to the foot of the bed and spread the top with a linen placemat from the Philippines. I have a poster of Alex Baumann in his Speedo, body tanned and shaved, taped to the inside of my closet door. He was Canada's flagbearer at the 1984 Olympics, where he won gold in the 200m and 400m individual medley, setting world records in both. I know his coach calls him Sasha, and he wears an earring. I imagine him kissing me while we are both wearing racing suits. I hadn't kissed anyone at that point, having botched my first chance with a swimmer named Erich on the roller coaster at Canada's Wonderland. I had to wait two years before I got another.

The poster makes Baumann look like a movie-star good guy, handsome and sweet. Luke Skywalker. But I am in awe of Victor Davis. Han Solo. I saw him once, at a big meet when I was fourteen. I remember a huge, hulking upper body and dark curly hair. It was like beholding a lion, the illumination of physical power, something both angry and contained rolling off and out of him.

Victor Davis was raised by his father in Guelph, Ontario, and trained his entire career with one coach, Cliff Barry, a soft-voiced, sturdily built former water polo Olympian. Davis was indisputably handsome, strong, disciplined, and famous for his fiercely competitive nature. He would use psychological terrorism in the ready room before races, staring down his competitors. With a towel over his head he'd shadowbox his way to the block, and might spit into the lane next to his. His most notorious moment came at the 1982 Common-wealth Games, when, in anger at a relay disqualification, he kicked over a plastic chair in front of Queen Elizabeth. He is the closest Canada has to a John McEnroe.

A 1983 documentary, *The Fast and the Furious*, presents Baumann as the Fast, Davis as the Furious. When I ask my old coach Byron about Davis and Baumann, he rattles off a number of arcane facts, that Davis swam poorly in odd years—'81, '83, '85, '87—and well in even ones, breaking world records in 1982 and 1984. Byron explains that Baumann and Davis were buddies, but that if Alex was the speedboat, Victor was the barge; he further compares Victor to a snowplow or a sixteen-cylinder Jaguar. Baumann and Davis were both tall, Davis just a hair shorter. Byron tells me that Davis was never described as a natural, the way Baumann was, that he considered strategy unnecessary but was a brilliant racer, a technically perfect swimmer, who never got caught from behind.

In a Montreal street in 1989, Davis, on foot, flung a bottle of orange soda at a black Honda Civic driven by a man who had been pestering Davis's girlfriend. The Honda accelerated, hit him straight-on and sped off. Davis, twenty-five, was comatose for two days before he died in hospital. The driver of the car served four months in prison.

Mary L. sits up in the dark and looks at me.

"Why are you breathing like that?"

"I'm visualizing."

She rolls over. I turn onto my back and do mini snow angels in the sheets.

Weeks later, bored in French class, I'll put my head on my desk and rub my prickly forearms against my cheek and try to stay awake.

OTHER SWIMMERS

Aidan gives me his U2 *War* T-shirt, unlaundered, and I keep it that way. Before I got it I was mortified by body odor, but I sniff the shirt possessively as, day by day, the smell fades alongside Aidan's interest in me.

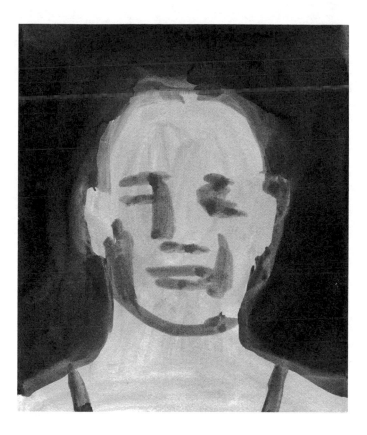

I befriend Kate, who moisturizes her hands so much
they glisten, and wears her hair pulled into a small,
high bun on the top of her head. Between sets, she gets
out and stands in the open double doors of the pool.
The billowing steam rushes past her into the frozen
parking lot and beyond that to the blue fields, train
tracks, and breaking winter morning.

During team meetings, when his name is called or
he has a question, Misha will raise his fist, index and
pinkie extended. He's into straightedge punk, writes
"H/C/T/O" (Hardcore Toronto) in marker on the
back of his hand, and wears black concert T-shirts
while the rest of us wear the team uniform.

I am not crazy about Stacy since noticing that she copied onto her own shoes the piano keys I drew on the inside of my sneakers.

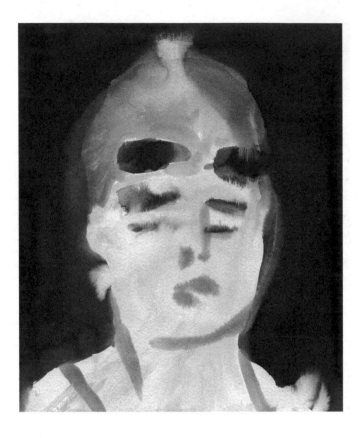

Mina wears earrings when she races. Christine has an attractive overbite, and her large, well-formed head looks good in a swim cap. I think Renata, who has dark eyebrows and wavy Zelda Fitzgerald hair, brassy and greenish from chlorine, is the prettiest girl on the team.

When I drive past the last house on the edge of a suburban development and see the windowless expanse of brick and aluminum siding, I think of Peter with the perfectly parted hair. He was small and kind (he gave me a Kit Kat once), and he always asked me to dance at the Saturday-night parties in his basement. His family owned two shar-peis.

Colleen is skinny, but I overhear Julia saying she has
"smiley butt." When I ask what that means, Julia says
her butt cheeks, when they poke out of the back of her
suit, look like they're smiling. After that I avoid Julia. I
don't warm to Colleen either after she announces, out
of the blue, how good two-percent milk tastes on her
cereal after drinking only skim for a year.

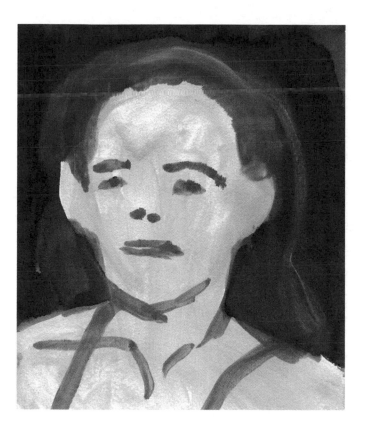

At a meet in Bradford, Ontario, Deena writes
"BARCELONA '92" on her back and down her arms.

As I'm sitting in the bleachers, stuck in a stare toward the pool, a swimmer from another team climbs up the bleachers beside me and puts his hand absentmindedly on my shoulder as he steadies himself past.

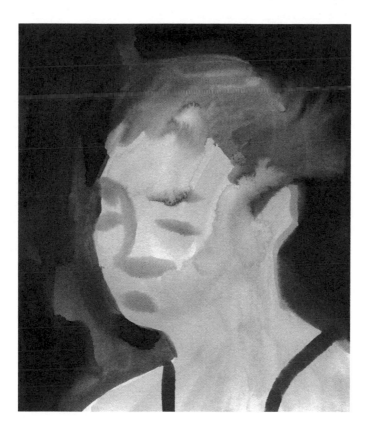

Mary K.'s father works at Apple, and a lot of her clothes have the bitten-Macintosh emblem on them. Mary L. leaves her pastel underwear hanging on a peg in the locker room, crotch exposed. I notice Mary S.'s armpit hair the same day I notice my own. Practicing dives, I tuck my arms behind my ears and glance sideways at my coach from the block.

Stan tells me that you can check if your breath is okay
by licking your forearm and smelling it.

At a meet I see a woman in the showers, soaping her body, completely naked, with a white tampon string dangling between her legs. I shower with my suit on, startled by nipples and pubic hair. My prudish edges are eventually buffered down by my teammates. At one meet Nuala yanks a paper-wrapped tampon from her duffel, waves it in circles like a magician's wand, and hollers: "Time to pull de plug!"

Agnes has paper-white skin, long red hair, and a deep voice. She is sarcastic and talks back to her coach. We swim the same events, and I want to be faster than her. She holds me off for a year before I start to beat her.

While two of our teammates swim a long-distance event, Jen and I pull on their track pants and wide, dirty sneakers, zip up their parkas—*Joe* and *Conrad* embroidered on the shoulders—pull the damp hoods low over our heads, and walk quickly through the men's locker room. Afraid to raise my head, I see only bare feet and more wide, dirty sneakers.

Ian was the first one to wear mittens on the pool deck like the swimmers from UCLA.

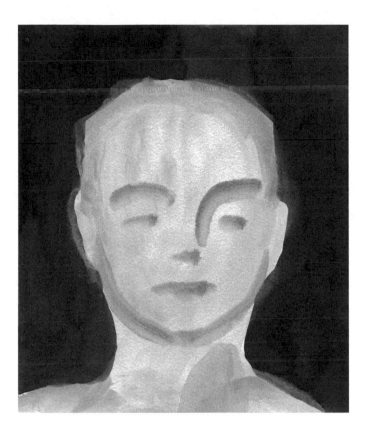

Jon and Desmond play with a stopwatch, trying to get
as low a time as possible by starting and immediately
stopping the clock. They have both hit the same
plateau, 00:00:05. I once did 00:00:03, but I stay
silent, watching from the corner of my eye. After two
minutes I pull off my headphones and wind the cord
around my Walkman. Jon holds out the stopwatch:
"You want a go?"

STUDEBAKERS

When I was six, my mother bought my father a giant chocolate-chip cookie for his birthday. She had the bakery pipe *To My Studebaker Nut with Love* on it in chocolate icing. There is a picture of my brother, my father, and me on the chesterfield, gathered around it, mouths gaping, as though we are about to take huge bites of it.

Before Derek and I start to swim, our family holidays are planned around car meets. My father, an active member of the Ontario Chapter of the Studebaker Drivers Club, packs us into his white 1964 Gran Turismo Hawk, the 1963 Raymond Loewy Avanti, or my favorite, a graceful green 1953 Champion Starliner Coupe, with mothballs rolling back and forth across the parcel shelf, and drives south to the States. I watch as the landscape changes from Canadian to American, watch the brick houses become wooden ones, watch the signage crank up in volume, the sidewalks buckle. I prop my legs on the cooler in the backseat and sniff my knees, or sit cross-legged, lean back, and stare up at the perforated white leather of the car ceiling, until the dots float millimeters from my eyeballs. Our summer weekends are spent walking up and down chrome rows of vintage cars, parked tidily on grassy lawns. Sometimes Derek and I play with American children in red and blue Studebaker Drivers Club T-shirts identical to ours.

I feel deep boredom most of the time, the boredom of being small and herded, the boredom of backseats, and the boredom of chrome car parts, displayed on the grass or in greasy lumps on tables made of sawhorses and doors. I get a strange feeling when I see, in the window of a gleaming Studebaker Lark, a pink card that coyly pleads: *Please don't fondle my parts . . .*

My father promises to buy me a 1957 candy-apple-red Corvette if I win an Olympic gold medal. In the corner of our dining room he keeps his collection of Matchbox cars, Studebaker Dinky Toys, and other small trinkets in a six-foot-tall display case. When it's plugged in, it rotates, shelves illuminated, the cars driving clockwise in a slow loop. The Timex sign that once crowned the top has been replaced by one that reads *STUDEBAKER* in tidy blue Helvetica. After dinner I like to lie on my side and watch the driverless parade.

In the spring of 2010, James and I live in Berkeley for a few weeks, while he works on a farming project. I buy a ten-session adult swim card for an outdoor public swimming pool near our rented house. Every morning at seven, I pull on my suit and jog over for the seven-thirty lap swim.

This morning it is raining steadily, making the surface of the water pocked and opaque. When I breathe to my right going up the pool, and left back down, I see a black chair at the side. Someone has spray-painted green loop-de-loops on its padded backrest. The pool has a wide concrete deck, surrounded by stubby pines and a chain-link fence woven through with green plastic ribbon. I take my kickboard from the end of the lane and lift my goggles onto my forehead. Two swimmers occupy each of the six lanes. The Berkeley Aquatics masters coach, who keeps inviting me to practice with his team, stands at the shallow end in rubber boots and a long red parka, holding a green-and-yellow-striped umbrella. He competed for the Moroccan national team and plays North African music from a boom box while he watches his swimmers. The steam coming off the water's surface is thin; it skims down the lane and blows east. As I kick I watch the masters swimmers train. I complete four hundred yards kicking, then switch to four hundred pull.

The pool is twenty-five yards long; an adjustment for me, a Canadian, whose default settings tend to metric. I overhear two women in the showers talking about the weather and have no sense of what forty degrees means. I competed in a few twenty-five-yard pools as a teenager, as Studebaker meets were slowly eclipsed by swim meets. One in Rochester, New York, another at an outdoor pool in Lakewood, Ohio, and the last one in the Robert J. H. Kiphuth Exhibition Pool at Yale. Unpacking after a move, I find a videotape my father made at the swim meet in Rochester, in 1987. The indoor pool is tiled in dark yellow and green, the windows are high and let in a bright but milky light. The camera finds me at one end of the pool. I am thirteen, narrow and tall. I pace behind the blocks before a race, adjusting the straps of my green and blue suit over and over again. As the other swimmers step to the blocks, it appears I am the only girl in the race.

As I swim, my father's video camera follows my progress up and down the pool. He uses the camera's timer, and the white digital numbers clock my pace at the bottom of the screen. It is a two-hundred-yard swim. My mother's voice, nearby, is cheering in a loud, almost panicky cry. I win easily, and rudely hop out of the pool before the other competitors finish. My father's camera zooms in slowly on my shiny head while I wrap myself in a towel and wipe my face dry. I pull on one of the green T-shirts the team made for the meet. Silk-screened in white, they say: *Mississauga-Rochester Invitational 1987, Hasta La Vista Baby!*

The tape stops, then starts again with a sweeping shot across the deck to Mrs. Mitchell. She is the mother of Luann and Daniel, who practice with Derek and me. Mrs. Mitchell sits in a plastic chair against the pool wall in her team T-shirt, staring at the water and rubbing her feet together distractedly. She notices the camera and makes a "Ta-da" flourish, grinning. The camera doesn't move. She looks away, smiling self-consciously. The camera remains on her.

Suddenly we're outside in the parking lot, beside our green Dodge van. The microphone catches the loud sound of the wind over bits of chipper conversation. The camera finds my mother talking to a small group of other mothers.

"Lorna!" my father calls.

She turns, smiles squinting in the sun, and waves. The other women look and wave too, and then make parting remarks and move away. Following them as they disperse, the camera finds Mrs. Mitchell as she makes her way through the parked cars, and zooms in. She waves and steps behind our green van, gesturing "Cut" with her hands. "It's not on!" My father laughs, then asks, "When are you going to come over to our place to watch?"

Mrs. Mitchell demurs, head tilted. "When are you going to come over to *our* place to watch?"

The tape stops. Then starts again as the camera turns to

the pool building, where Derek and I have emerged in matching Levi's jean jackets with matching sleeves rolled up. The camera zooms in, making us blurry, then clear. I walk straight up to it and ask my father through the lens:

"Can we go to Ames? They have Jams."

I receive no response.

"Come on, can we go to Ames? Please? There are no Ameses in Canada."

I plead and plead with the lens. The camera turns away and finds my brother, arms crossed, leaning against the van. My whining continues off camera as my father zooms in on Derek (blurry, clear), who is in a bad mood after swimming poorly. Derek asks the camera if we're going to a restaurant. The tape stops and my screen dissolves into snow.

As I rewind the tape I remember that we didn't go to a restaurant; the two teams met at somebody's house for a poolside barbecue. At one point I set aside my paper plate and asked to use the bathroom. I was shown to an outdoor cabana structure, wallpapered in a yellow and brown palm-tree-and-toucan pattern. There was a wooden lacquered sign hanging on the wall beside the sink that read: *Don't piss in our pool; we don't swim in your toilet.*

ETOBICOKE

Derek has a record called "The Song of the Humpback Whale" that came tucked into the back cover of one of his nature books. It's pressed onto a thin, floppy piece of red plastic, so he puts it on top of another 45 to play. After lunch, Derek and I lie on our stomachs in the living room, listening to the deep keening and moaning of the whales. After a half-hour, we go swimming.

Derek is nine and I am seven. We're playing a game we call "Shipwreck": after being shipwrecked in the ocean, we have been swimming for days and are near death. There is an island within sight, but we are tiring fast. We begin the game ten feet from the edge of the Serson pool deck.

"I see land—don't give up!"

Derek, neck lolling in the water:

"I don't know if I'm going to make it. . . ."

As we approach the side of the pool we weaken.

"I can't make . . . gluplup . . ."

"I can't make it."

"Plup glup . . . I can't, I can't, I can't . . ."

"I feel so cold . . ."

"No. Don't give up, we're almost there!"

I try to help Derek by pulling his arms. They splash, and flail out of my grasp.

"Go on without me . . . save yourself. . . ."

In the deep end, a chubby sunburnt girl dives off the springboard, followed by a tanned teenager in cutoff jeans. Waiting for a turn is an East Indian boy who does tidy back-flips. Behind him is a pale man wearing a cross on a thin chain. He folds his arms across his chest and whips his long hair back to get it out of his face; his girlfriend stands behind him, and he talks to her without turning around. He's working on his cannonball. She has a skinny blond wet ponytail pointing stiffly down. She tugs at the bottom of her one-piece and holds her nose when she jumps. Her friend, who doesn't get her hair wet, watches from the side of the pool, feet kicking in the water, ankles crossed.

We are now a foot from the side of the pool. Our arms reach for the painted blue wall and concrete lip and try to grip it, but keep slipping back into the water. This goes on for twenty minutes until we hoist ourselves out and lie on our backs, panting dramatically. A lifeguard looks at us from his chair and then at the other lifeguard directly opposite. The two guards mirror each other, both arms on the armrests, feet flat on the platform. They wear identical dark aviator sunglasses and have whistles strung through their yellow tank tops. Derek finds a wide, shallow puddle of water that has been heating up in the July sun and sits in it. I find a dry expanse of pale deck and pull my knees to my chest, moving over every minute to look back at the butterfly-shaped mark my wet suit bottom has left on the concrete. After ten minutes we jump back into the water and begin Shipwreck anew. The deep twanging boom of the rebounding diving board carries across the park for hours until the pool is cleared at six and the water flattens, plate smooth.

At night, in bed, when we hear the board booming again, we know: pool hoppers. Bad kids, smokers, heavy metalers, trespassers needing forgiveness. I was afraid of them the way I was afraid of breaking any rules, of anything that smelled like cigarettes. Nineteen years later, about twelve miles east of Serson pool, two friends named Jason and I scale the chain-link fence on a hot June night. Sunnyside–Gus Ryder pool is on the shore of Lake Ontario. Riding a sugar high of birthday cake and white wine, we dive in fully clothed, the Jasons in their shorts, me in a pink party dress.

Visiting my brother and his family in Toronto, I use the washroom and see, draped over the side of the bathtub, a gray towel, the words *Etobicoke Swim Club* and a moiréd maple leaf emblazoned across it in fading burgundy. I dry my hands and go downstairs.

"I know what I want for Christmas from you," I tell Derek.

"What? It's February."

"My ESC towel. You never even swam for them!"

"It needs washing."

"Fine!"

My sister-in law overhears us.

"I think I delivered Emmett on that towel."

By the time I join the Etobicoke Pepsi Swim Club in the fall of 1988, Derek has quit swimming. I swim well at the second 1988 Olympic trials, finishing eleventh and thirteenth in my best events, and my coach suggests I change clubs. It used to be called the Etobicoke Swim Club, or ESC, but after a few swimmers made it to the podium at the Seoul Olympics, it has attracted a corporate sponsor. Mitch, the new head coach, was recruited from the University of Florida. He is an Olympian, has coached Olympians. Mitch looks like Dennis Quaid, wears a dark leather bomber jacket with a sheepskin collar, and drinks can after can of Diet Coke during morning practices.

The Etobicoke Olympium swimming pool feels cathedral. The hulky proportions of a fifty-meter indoor pool inspire hushed humility, the concrete diving tower like an altar (with occasional plummeting cruciforms). Mitch plays Rod Stewart over the synchronized swimmers' underwater sound system, drowning out whatever music we have in our own heads (Nuala, Erasure; Claude, U2; Marcel, R.E.M.; me, the Cure).

The transition from my smaller team to Etobicoke Pepsi is steep. Stricter rules, longer, more difficult practices, and tougher, more serious swimmers. I practiced in the faster lanes with my old team, but here I'm in the slowest. I dread swimming in lane eight, where a dark window of mirrored glass stretches along the pool wall, seven feet below the surface. It's like swimming past the mouth of a cave. I worry that someone's there, watching, and feel a jolt of panic if I catch any sort of reflection in the window. Being one of the slower practice swimmers is crushing, and the cross-training—miles of running through the suburbs and along the service roads surrounding the pool, endless steps up the side of a man-made hill—is lonely. Not a great runner, I can't keep up, and I jog desperately, miserably, a half-hour or more behind everyone else, tears welling, sides cramping. I look down as I run, watching the jerky progress of patchy-crabgrass curbs while the indifferent gray noise of normal life whizzes above along the sweeping Etobicoke overpasses.

Despite my misery, I get dramatically faster in the first few months. The graduation to higher national rankings, the intensity of Mitch's coaching, and inclusion on an elite team give me a feeling of security, pride, and purpose, a feeling slightly deflated by having to borrow, for big meets, a sample set of the expensive team uniform. It is too big, so I roll the track bottoms and jacket sleeves up. I'm careful with the sample: I fold it neatly, take it off to eat, knowing I have to return it when we get home.

The Olympium pool is bisected by a white bulkhead during the twenty-five-meter short-course season, but for long-course training we roll it slowly across the pool to the deep end at the top of morning practice. Three or four boys bend over each end, a mini Iwo Jima tableau in dry double-layered trunks, making sure the motion is even and the bulkhead doesn't jam diagonally across the width. One girl per lane sits atop, guiding the loosened lane ropes over the bulkhead as it moves slowly along. The ropes are retightened with a heavy winch, which will often slip into the water and sink to the bottom. I'm grateful for this prep, a reprieve before the sentence of practice.

The interior of the Olympium hums in the mornings, the aural scale amplified by the density of the chlorinated air over the water's surface. Mid-practice we do lungbusters, fifty meters underwater. We push off at one end and glide, then kick soundlessly through the blue. At the far end we release the air in our lungs, and our bubbles rush up in a muffled crash. As our heads break the surface, the pool echoes with our breathing. The whole process is overseen by the silent sweep of the pace clock swallowing time, rest, and seconds of air before we inhale and slip under again.

On the phone one night I ask my brother if he was bothered when I swam faster than he did.

"You were as fast as me when I quit and you swam at Etobicoke Pepsi after, so it was natural you'd be faster. It didn't bother me, it made sense, you were better at it, way more into it." He pauses. "I was proud of you. I practiced a couple of times with your group, but the guys were dicks. The stoners I swam with were cooler. They listened to the best music."

We talk for a bit about Rhys and Christian, two brothers in Intermediate Age Group who had stratospherically better taste than we did in clothes and music.

"It was easy for me to quit," Derek reasons. "My last race was the hundred free at a provincial meet. I swam a best time but my shoulders hurt so much I couldn't lift myself out of the pool." He laughs. "I think I disqualified our relay team at that meet too."

The weight room is in the basement of the Etobicoke Olympium athletic complex. It's a small room, with cinderblock walls painted a glossy pale yellow. From the pocked panels of the dropped ceiling, fluorescent light bears down bluish-white and cold. The door suctions shut over gray industrial carpet. The women's team does weight training three nights a week in addition to resistance tubing and running, and we record our progress in messy columns of numbers and capitalized titles—LATS, DIPS, DELTS, CURLS, SQUATS, PRESS—our photocopied chart pages growing smudgy and dog-eared over the course of a month. The room has a specific smell: of steel weights, grease, dried sweat, old carpet, and vinyl padded benches. It is a salty, ferrous odor, strongest during hamstring pulls, when my face is mashed into the sparkly blue bench.

One night, we are listening to a mixed tape as we go through the circuit. When "In the Air Tonight" begins, somebody switches off the light. Everyone stops, the squeaking and clanking gently cease. Nobody speaks. We sit quietly in the dark, listening to the song. All I can see are the tiny red lights glowing on the tape deck and the motionless shapes of the other girls in the room.

This was around the time Miriam's father died. One afternoon she didn't come to practice. Mitch sat us all down on the deck afterward and told us that her father had been killed in an accident. She didn't attend any practices for a week. When she came back her face looked tired and her skin was pale. Sometimes she started crying in the water, holding on to the side of the pool. Her friends didn't leave her by herself. I was still new, not close to anyone on the team, but Miriam was kind to me. We swam the same event and I was slightly faster, which now left me with an uneasy feeling.

Miriam is in the weight room that night. I see her nearby, hugging her knees to her chest. Nothing is said once the song ends, but the mood is low. Somebody turns the lights back on, and we quickly finish up, shower, change, and leave. I wonder if that song meant something to Miriam. My mother picks me up.

"Tired?"

"Yeah." I keep my eyes closed on the drive home.

There is a covered plate on the kitchen counter. Beneath the foil are a pork chop, green beans, and some mashed potato.

Next to the plate is a small saucer of gravy, covered in Saran wrap.

I drop my bag in the hall and hang my parka on the banister. A single place is set at the dining room table. As my mother heats up the gravy, I pour myself a glass of milk and sit down. In the dark living room, my father is listening to CBC Radio. He's stretched out on his back, six-foot-one along the length of the brown chesterfield, and his arm is slung across his eyes. He turns the lights out and the volume up loud when he listens to the radio. He does this with movies on TV too, turns off every light in the house and turns the volume way up. My mother brings the gravy to the table and I let it cool a little while I stare into space, listening to the familiar radio-host voices—Barbara Budd and Mary Lou Finlay—from my chair, sipping my milk.

My mother's noises come from the kitchen. The fridge opens and closes and opens and closes. I hear the dishwasher start. I chew my chop and scoop my potatoes. I wonder if Derek is in his room, and I picture him: he'll be either at his desk doing homework or sitting on his bed, his shoulders against the wall and his feet straight out in front of him. He reads like this, or with the book propped up on his chest, using the bottom half of his glasses. He has been reading science fiction and fantasy lately, lots of Isaac Asimov and Larry Niven. I like the cover and title of his paperback copy of *A Wrinkle in Time*. I finish my dinner, wash my plate, and go upstairs to find my duffel bag at the foot of my bed. The wet towels and suits have been hung up in the bathroom. I walk into Derek's room, where I find him pretty much as imagined, on his bed, propped up against the wall, reading science fiction.

"Hey."

"Hey."

He doesn't look up.

"What is the name of that Phil Collins song, the one that goes: 'I can feel it coming in the air tonight, oh lord'?"

"How should I know?" He's still not looking up. Then he sighs. "I really dislike Phil Collins."

I pick at a sticker on his chest of drawers.

"Mnh."

Derek ignores me. I stick my tongue out at his drawers, then go back to my room. There is French homework in my school bag that I consider doing but know I can cram in during the disorganized five minutes before class starts. I change into a purple Snoopy nightshirt and go to the bathroom to brush my teeth.

DEREK

After my nephews are tucked into bed and while Derek is working, my sister-in-law, Kristin, and I eat some brownies we made, and wash them down with red wine. I had gone to a party the night before, and as I tell Kristin about it I remember that I stopped in at a swim meet.

I'm wearing a dress, heels. The brightly lit U of T pool is on my way, and I look in through the ground-level windows. A swim meet. Finals. I go inside. Shaggy's version of "Angel of the Morning" echoes across the vaulted space. The first few swimmers dive in to warm up, breaking the plate surface with a churning flutter kick. More swimmers, wearing extra suits for drag, stand at one end as their coaches give warm-up sets. Families in the gallery sip coffees and Cokes, flip through programs. The air is warm and heavy, steaming the dark windows. I find a seat and take off my coat.

Twenty minutes into warm-up the music gets louder. The water is bobbing with team caps. One lane all green and a few yellow, another lane all white and red. Collisions during warm-up are inevitable: swimmers from opposing teams forced to share a lane take out their aggression in impatient glares, or pass each other with quick, vicious flip turns. The din grows, and the wet tile shimmers with unwinding, expectant energy. Sprints begin in the outside lanes. Coaches—hands cupped around their chins—start their swimmers off the blocks, ten seconds apart.

A long whistle indicates the end of warm-up, and the surface returns to a glassy sheet. My cell phone buzzes in my coat pocket. A few races are swum; then the women's 100 meter freestyle final is announced. Each competitor is named, and at lane four, the announcer remarks on the woman's age: thirty-five. My age. I strain to hear her name and remember it from 1992. She has cropped blond hair, the slim hips and ropy build of a long-term athlete. I watch her pull on her cap, think the obvious thoughts, make the obvious comparisons. The woman looks good, fast, and she stands apart from the swimmers flanking her. Her demeanor is serious. She reminds me of a swimmer who practiced with our team in 1992, Kylie. She was in her mid-thirties then, and among the top five in the country.

Kylie would sometimes room with a female coach at out-of-town meets. I wonder how it felt for her to be surrounded by us—flinging pancakes around the restaurant while she sipped tea. Girls who wiped snot gleefully on one another, who were closing in on her records. There were older men too—talented swimmers who'd immigrated from Eastern Europe with their wives and children, and who didn't goof around.

At televised meets, the commentators' boomy, magnanimous voices declare any woman over twenty-seven a "veteran." As she approaches the blocks they mention her age, some details of her life, a mother who is ill, a deferral to a top law school, adult sacrifices. Then the name of the woman in the next lane will be announced. The one looking to catch her, the one to watch.

The older woman wins her race and offers a graceful, tight smile. She punches the air quickly, but the punch seems private. I watch her lift herself out of the pool. Despite the busy deck, she looks alone. I pull on my coat and push out into the Toronto night.

. . .

The morning after the brownies, Derek wakes up early with his three boys, and hearing them through the walls, I wake up too. I lie there, easily, happily, listening to him talk to his sons, and I imagine a version of my own life had I stayed in that city, stuck with that boyfriend, and staked out a little front yard in Toronto's leafy streets. It's a nice life. My stomach grumbles and I remember the time Derek and I planned a night raid on our parents' kitchen the year of the renovation.

I'm eleven, Derek is thirteen, and we share a bedroom while plastic sheets and spackled drywall make new shapes in our house. We prepare our raid carefully, trace our path to memorize the few creaking stairs and leave the spring-lock cupboards ajar. We test the batteries of the Maglites we will carry in our pajama pockets.

Derek sets the alarm on his calculator watch for three a.m. When it goes off he complains into his pillow that he is too sleepy. I insist, bug-eyed, that we stick to the plan. When we get to the kitchen, we realize there isn't much to raid. The jackpot: a box of granola bars. I take two of them and Derek quietly snaps two bananas off a bunch. He reaches into a cupboard and pulls out a bag of *tuyo*—dried, salted fish from the

Filipino grocery—and holds it up in the halo of my Maglite, grinning.

In our room, we place the food on Derek's bedspread. Derek takes a banana and I take a granola bar. We eat our healthy snacks quietly, on our sides, under our covers.

Back in New York, I wake at four a.m. and can't get back to sleep. I put the kettle on and let the dog out. With the oven preheating, I scrounge for chocolate and butter. I find half an ingot of Scharffen Berger in the fridge and twelve individually wrapped squares of Ghirardelli in the cupboard. Just the amount I need. I start melting the chocolate, I let the dog in, and he watches from across the kitchen floor while I mix butter and sugar. I taste a fingertip of it from the side of the bowl.

The melting chocolate turns a lighter, shining shade of brown. I was envious of my brother's hazel eyes, and I told him so once. He said that he'd rather have brown ones like mine. It blew my preteen mind that after I looked up to him for everything, he'd want something I had.

As I scrub a dirty pan in the sink, I get the fishy whiff of last night's halibut. It brings me suddenly to the edge of a dock on Lake Ontario: a dark spring school night when my father took us to the waterfront park to watch the smelt dipping. I ran up and down the dock in my brother's rubber boots, "helping" my dad and other dads scoop the tiny silvery fish from the black water. We lugged a reeking white plastic bucketful home to my mom. The body of a classmate's father would be found off the same dock a few years later. I think about this, and about the bottle of opalescent pink nail polish that classmate once gave me, as I crack three eggs and a yolk into a bowl and beat them with a fork. I remember that that classmate, in fifth grade, played Estragon in the Toronto Young People's Theatre production of *Waiting for Godot*.

I knock a bag of sugar to the floor, spilling it. There's still some clumsy sleep in my limbs as I wipe up the mess. For a brief moment I consider scooping the crystals into my mouth with a spoon, the way I did when I started swimming.

My tooth is always sweetest in the mornings. When I swam I was attuned to appetite and fatigue in a way I probably never will be again. I spent hours submerged, holding my breath, deprived of taste, scent, sound, and most sight. After practice I'd stare into the fridge, looking for leftovers, and sneak slices of butter. If I was sent to the kitchen to fetch something, I'd stick a soup spoon in the sugar bowl and then into my mouth before returning to the table.

I'd forgo all dessert and candy in the two weeks leading up to a big competition. It was part of my tapering routine—my coach would build in less difficult practices for those of us competing, so I would try to restrict my sugar intake to design a bigger rush during the meet. It was more superstition than nutrition, a mini Lent before my races. I still tend to consume sugar when my body is at a threshold.

Derek didn't have the same cravings; he could make his February birthday box of Toffifee chocolates last until Halloween.

I clean the countertop and put ingredients away. My cupboards, seen through the eyes of a kitchen raider, are groaning. Boxes of crackers, bags of nuts, a butter-biscuit Ritter Sport, maraschino cherries, a jar of Nutella, a box of organic peanut butter cookies. Derek and I abandoned the raids when we moved back into our separate rooms. Then he took a trip to Germany with my dad and his college students, and returned taller and cooler.

When Derek gets his driver's license he reluctantly agrees to help my mother drive me to my morning practices. He slouches down to the kitchen, pajama legs sticking out of the bottoms of his jeans, grabs the keys to the station wagon. Backing out of the driveway he puts on a tape, which, in my memory, is always Billy Bragg's *Talking with the Taxman About Poetry*. The car warms and my brother turns up the stereo volume.

The drive feels like a movie. We don't talk; we just listen to the lyrics, to the guitar—loud, plangent—and watch Mississauga landmarks pass. An amputated lighthouse, the cornstarch factory. The funeral home where we once stared into our next-door neighbor's open casket, Port Credit marina, Pizza Pizza. I long to say something to Derek as a friend, an equal, to dissolve the feeling that I am a child needing a ride, but can't think of anything. We have less in common since he quit swimming. I took it up because he did, so when he quit, I wondered if he knew something I didn't. I inspect the tape case in the dashboard light and sniff the liner notes. Blueberries.

We loop the Burger King drive-thru. Derek orders: coffee and a Croissan'wich. I order the only thing I can think of: hot chocolate, separating us even further in age.

The road gets hilly as we pass wealthier neighborhoods. Porcupine Avenue, Tennyson Avenue. A talented butterflyer named Doug, who has long blond bangs and will become a Buddhist, lives there, as does Duncan, whom I have a thing for. In a year I'll spend a blissful hour sharing headphones with Duncan on a drive back from Ottawa. We'll listen to Billy Bragg then too. I'll drape my arms over the back of his seat, one arm on his shoulder, my fingers brushing the front of his T-shirt as the van jostles us. In three years he'll kiss me at a Billy Bragg concert and my feelings for him will fade.

I was always watching Derek for signs of what was possible, how to make decisions, what to like and how to tell. I knew he wanted to lose me, and I tried to keep my distance, but I wore the same Converse All Stars as he did, the same jeans. I was a smaller, androgynous version of him, except I was starting to like shoulder pads. Around this time we got our family portrait done at The Bay Portrait Studio. When we returned to pick out our photo package, the clerk gestured to a picture of me and my brother and said, "Here's a nice one of the two boys."

We turn back onto Lakeshore Road. Derek takes two huge bites of his sandwich, offers a bite to me, finishes it in four. At a stoplight, I roll down my window and pour an inch of my scalding hot chocolate out onto the pavement so I can drink it.

We pull up in front of the pool doors. I turn to him:

"Are you going to pick me up? Or is Mom?"

Derek shrugs.

"I hope you do."

He makes a face. "Why? I'm going back to sleep."

This time I shrug.

NIGHT KITCHEN

February 1987. At the 4:25 alarm my routine is this: From the bed, reach for the two damp swimsuits drying on the bedroom doorknob, take off my pajamas, and pull the suits on halfway. Under the covers, pull on track pants, three T-shirts, a sweatshirt, two pairs of socks, which have been piled at the foot of my bed the night before. Once dressed, switch on my bedside lamp.

The hour between four and five a.m. is dreadful, especially in the dead of Canadian winter. Knowing I have to get into a chilly, overchlorinated pool and endure two hours of unrelenting muscle pain makes it worse. The hour is redeemed by the quiet, the bluish-blackness out the window, less menacing than midnight dark. I ride, next to my mother, through our suburban streets, bundled into a team parka, listening to the tires squeak over the packed snow.

. . .

My mother's car. When Derek and I were in grade school, my mother worked Tuesdays and Thursdays. We would head to the public library at three-thirty and stay till it closed at six. The children's section had a picture window, where I'd watch for my mother's round Oldsmobile Cutlass headlights to turn onto Atwater Avenue. As I got older, I'd look for the wide, squarish beams of her Chevy Malibu station wagon to turn into the Terry Fox Memorial Pool parking lot, and then, a few years later, wait for her four-eyed Ford LTD to pull up to the Olympium doors.

Sometimes on those mornings, waiting for my mother to come downstairs, I make something I call a "muffin-in-a-mug": Quaker instant bran muffin mix, half a cup of milk, stirred, nuked for two minutes, and then eaten with a spoon. It will be half bready, half raw, but sweet and warm. I bring it along in the car if we are running late, spooning the stuff into my mouth with mittens on, as I watch the icy streetscapes swoosh past.

This was my ritual: I put the batter-filled mug in the microwave and set the time to 1:11:00, the time I want to swim the SC 100m breaststroke in 1987. Then I cover my eyes with one hand, finger on the start panel, imagining my starting block and the pool: a vast table of water, still and clear. I see the dirty grout between the small white tiles. The lane ropes pulled taut along the surface. I can hear teammates in the stands and families in the gallery. A long, sharp whistle calls us onto the blocks. The quiet is sudden. My hands reach to touch the front of the sandpapery block, between my toes.

I push Start on the microwave. Breathe, dive. In the kitchen, in my track pants, there are eight or nine strokes the first length, a two-handed touch, and silence again at the turn. I hear a faucet upstairs turn on, then off. In my mind I am ahead, no one in my periphery. My legs start to tire. I lay a hand on the countertop at fifty meters, knees and chest hurting. When I breathe I see the officials dressed in white at the end of the lanes, legs apart and hands behind their backs, looking grimly down into the pool. Halfway down the pool on my final length I hear sharp beeping and open my eyes—the microwave is flashing 00:00:00. Too slow by about five seconds.

Other times I prepare my mug, set the microwave to 1:11:00, and sit at the kitchen table with a glass of milk. I don't look at the timer. I look outside at the dark wooden deck and icy trees, I look at my knees in my gray track pants, I pick some lint off, I think about how I like my track pants to be either gray or, gun-to-head, navy blue. My mind wanders but maintains a loose grip on the seconds. When I sense the time is close I shut my eyes and imagine the last five or six strokes to the wall. I finish—imagine slamming my arms dramatically into the yellow touchpads—and look up at the microwave. Sometimes this works, but most of the time I'm too early. I watch the last numbers count down to 00:00:00, the light inside the oven clicks off, and the long beep indicates the time is up.

February 1991. I take my mountain bike out into the snow for a ride and, halfway down a steep hill, resolve to bicycle to my best friend Chris's house twenty-five kilometers away. The winter afternoon quickly blackens, and I am about three kilometers south when it starts to blizzard. I'm afraid of strangers who might stop to help me, so when I hear a car approach I hide behind a bank of plowed snow on the shoulder. I've been gone two hours. One car slows as I am ducking behind a frozen drift. I poke my head over the top. It is my father. I roll my bike out and over the bank, and he puts it in the back of his Suzuki Sidekick. I get in. We drive back silently. A few weeks later he asks if I think I might like to see a psychiatrist.

I haven't been swimming for two years, and am due at McGill University in the fall. During these years, I ping-pong between my age and my *swimming* age—the number that coaches, teammates, competitors, and I unconsciously and automatically consider in relation to Olympic years, to puberty, to age-group rankings, to height, weight, strength, and development. After quitting in 1989, I voraciously try to catch up on the rituals of being suburban sixteen, seventeen, filling my head with steep French literature and new music, notebooks with bad poetry, gut with crushes, sketchbooks with agonies of dragons, raccoons, and smudgy Gothic calligraphy. Chris and I write out an urgent vow—something about making the best comics and stories in the world—that we place in a peanut butter jar and bury on a slope beneath a boulder.

But after the long bus rides home from high school, I retreat to the basement in my shorts, loop a pair of surgical tubes around an iron pillar, set my stopwatch, and do an hour of resistance-band training. I listen to the thrum and squeak of the rubber and iron in the windowless room, sweating into the mustard-swirl carpet. I continue dry-land workouts like an automaton, simulating swimming in a basement on the edge of the Niagara Escarpment. I yank on the tubes hoping they might give me a clue—tell me what I'm doing—willing my swimming age to remember what it is capable of.

When I graduate from high school in May, my step-aunt Pamela, a glamorous, single career woman with no children, invites me and my friend Jane to stay with her for the summer, in a town outside Leeds, England.

From Pam's house, Jane and I take trains to the beach at Southampton, the National Museum of Photography, Film and Television in Bradford, the Brontë house in Haworth. We punt in Cambridge, stay in youth hostels. I start to long for larger experiences I have no idea how to acquire. At one hostel, in Brighton, I hear a young woman's voice beneath my window singing "Off to Dublin in the Green," heartbreakingly, drunkenly, and I have a feeling that things will be—as the song sounds—complicated, mostly sad, and mostly beautiful.

When the singing stops, I keep listening at the window from my bunk bed:

"Oy, Tracy, get me top off, it's all I got to wear tomorrow!"

"Surely you're joking."

"Nuh, I mean it, git it off! Do us a favor."

We stay with Jane's cousins in Birmingham, and she transforms: her Brummie accent emerges, her neckline scoops, her posture becomes defiant. She borrows their tight jeans, jerseys, and hair spray. I watch her, wearing a wool fisherman's sweater and vintage pajama bottoms, then go back to underlining my rancid paperbacks. At a campground in Ayr we part ways, planning to meet at Pam's in a week. I go to Edinburgh and Glasgow, eat spoonfuls of peanut butter on park benches. Jane returns to Birmingham, goes to clubs, and does a lot of drugs. Later, back on Pam's high, flowery-sheeted bed, Jane whispers that she slept with her cousin's friend. We shriek for a while; then I lie beside her in the dark as she snores softly.

Jane flies back to Canada the next day, and I stay on another few weeks with Pam. While she works, I sketch in her garden or take the bus into Leeds to walk around. It's different without Jane. We rifled through the charity shops, drank barley water in pubs, giddily went to see a band called the Pooh Sticks. I walk to the university pool and watch the City of Leeds swim team practice. The coach, Terry Denison, coached breaststrokers Adrian Moorhouse and Suki Brownsdon—names I know from the international rankings. I lean over the railing from the stands and listen to Denison give his swimmers sets.

From the window of the bus back to Pam's, I see a dark-haired man exit a door and turn a corner. He is wearing Adidas track pants, clean white sneakers, and a battered leather motorcycle jacket zipped snugly up to his chin. I decide I want to swim again, and I want to know where to get clothes like that.

Over fish fingers, Pam and I talk about my taking up swimming again. I decide to defer McGill, train for the next year, and live with my brother in downtown Toronto.

February 2010. During the last afternoon of a monthlong stay in London, I wander into a café adjoining a bookstore and eyeball the cakes. There are four, but two stand out. A dark cherry polenta cake, dense- and rich-looking, and a lemon olive-oil cake, shiny yellow with amber edges, flecked with spiky rosemary. I order a square of the latter, sit and eat it bite by slow bite, staring off into space, incredulous. When I finish, I interrupt the waitress as she clears my teacup, and stammer: "That cake . . ."

"Oh, I know, right?" She laughs. I ask her where the recipe came from, but she winks and will say only that it is a secret, "North African" in origin. I thank her (for nothing), pay and leave, but not before peering at the cake closely, trying to memorize its nature. Its defining qualities are a large crumb, a puckering tartness, olive-oily moisture, and a crunchy, sweet glaze that seems soaked through. The cake is coarse, and deep yellow in color.

Rising at four-thirty a.m. back in New York, I search online for "Lemon, olive oil cake, Morocco" and "Lemon cake, rosemary, olive oil." I frankenstein a recipe from five different sources in an attempt to conjure that London afternoon.

My night kitchen is clean, calm, and quiet. Outside, all is dark except for two windows in an apartment building opposite. I grease a cake pan, grate four lemons, and rub the rinds with sugar. The night kitchen is a changed place, its clicks and hums are louder, the pots and pans make a wincing clatter when I pull them out of the cupboard. The tapping of rain and the muffled whooping of police sirens are the only other sounds. I juice lemons and add half the liquid to the sugar, then whisk with three eggs.

After combining the dry ingredients, I add the sugar mixture and the olive oil, then pour the batter into the prepared cake pan and slide it into the oven. Next: the glaze. In a small saucepan I add a sprig of rosemary to the remaining lemon juice, and then sugar, bring this to a boil, add a blurp of agave nectar and, after a finger dip, the juice and grated rind of one more lemon. I let this steep while the cake bakes. As I wait, I make tea and read the previous day's paper, stopping to stare out the window at the changing light. I feel relief at a lightening sky. When I took up swimming again and joined the University of Toronto team in 1991, the practices were held in a fifty-meter pool with high, street-level windows on the west wall. I breathed to my right going up the lane, my left going down, and I'd watch the sky's colors mark the advancing time, turning from black to purple, then ultramarine, periwinkle, mauve, and finally, with warm-down, lungs aching, relief flooding, a cold, pale gray.

When the lemon cake is done, I perforate it all over with a fork and pour the glaze over it. I let it cool in the tin for half an hour, before turning it out onto a plate. When I do this, I see I've completely burned the bottom, so I slice the charred layer off and leave the cake to cool a little longer. Upon inspection, it seems to have the right color, but sampling it I know I'm off. Close, but off.

My mother comes to visit me in New York for a week. The quilt I fling across the guest room bed is coming apart, fraying at the edges. She insists on repairing it, so I lug my sewing machine out of the closet and set her up at the dining room table. As she mends the quilt, I ask her if it hurt her feelings when I asked her not to watch to me swim.

"I guess I thought it was a teenage thing," she says, looking over her glasses at a seam. "I wonder how old was I then?"

I walk to the kitchen to reheat some takeaway coffee and say over my shoulder, "I was around fourteen, so you must have been, what, forty-four?"

". . . but I might have watched anyway."

"What do you mean, you *might* have?" from the kitchen.

"If I wanted to see how you did, I'd watch from where you couldn't see me."

"You did?"

"Sneaky, huh?"

I watch the coffee heat and think about this. I smile.

Back in the dining room I hand her some coffee. "I never use that machine, but I will if you show me how to thread bobbins."

"Oh, that's easy," she says, "but you have to thread carefully, because if you don't it will go all *bohol-bohol*."

I ask her about the other swimmers' parents.

"I remember all of the other parents thought you were very pretty and very fast."

"Which were you more proud of?"

"Both."

During my wedding reception, my mother, dressed in a white toga with a garland crowning her head, performed a dance to Elvis's "Hawaiian Wedding Song." Her lips moved silently to the lyrics as she swayed around me and James, perched on a coffee table. She gracefully placed leis around our necks. At the conclusion of her dance, as the applause was petering, she bowed and cried out, "See! Leanne's not the only talented one!" Everyone laughed, but I exchanged a quick glance with James. What? He looked back at me, eyes wide.

At the end of her visit I wake my mother early to drive her to the train station. She throws back the covers when I whisper to her; her limbs—in the dark, in her underwear—look like my own. Earlier in the week she borrowed a dress of mine to go to the *Glamour* Women of the Year Awards; she tried on several before deciding on a vintage black and yellow one. I was both reassured and weirded out that they all fit and suited her, even though her body is a different shape, and much shorter than mine.

Downstairs the blue light filters through the windowpanes as I put the kettle on, and make weak, milky tea for her Pirelli thermos. When we step outside, the air has a thin, mauve cast, is cold as lake water.

TRAINING CAMP

Barbados, the last week of December 1991. I am sharing a hotel room with Rachel, Erin, and Shelley. I don't sleep well the first night; it is hot and I can hear "Smells Like Teen Spirit" from the hotel behind ours. I stare at the curly iron bars of the open bedroom window and think to myself: That is the hotel where normal people stay, normal people just a little older than us. They are listening to Nirvana and staying up late and drinking killer Kool-Aid and eating Doritos.

"A mosquito / My libido."

I lie on my side and wait for the weak wheeze of the fan to reach me. The hotel has given each room an oscillating upright fan, and I'm the farthest away from it, behind Shelley, who smells like insect repellent and shampoo. The fan pushes fainter notes of chlorine, suntan lotion, and wet concrete around the room.

Training camp takes place between Christmas and the

New Year. We get up at 5:45 a.m., and gather on the lawn at 5:50. It's dark, and the Caribbean insects are loud. As we wait, we stretch out on the cool grass and use our duffel bags as pillows. We're sleepy, skin still hot from yesterday's sun, our hoods pulled up against the morning chill. I see the lumpy outlines of my teammates on the lawn.

Their bodies are familiar. Since nothing is concealed in a swimsuit, no size or shape, the thrilling reversal is to see bodies clothed: obscured lines of muscle and limb, how someone tucks or untucks, cuffs ankles or pockets hands. I like the way the boys look dry, wrapped in long sleeves and track pants, hair brushed and parted, like the Morrissey song. From the lawn we can hear the ocean over the road. At 5:50, Byron and Linda cross the damp grass and unlock the doors of the minivans. Everyone piles in, and we jostle against windows and one another while the vans climb the road to the pool. A fresh breeze comes through the windows, and the sound of surf recedes. Nobody talks; everyone wants to be immobile for a little longer.

When we arrive at the Barbados Aquatic Centre, the lights are off. The pool is fifty meters long, sitting smack in the middle of a large field. It is surrounded on three sides by loud billboard advertising, eight feet high. Even in the dark, the Barbadian colors are bright. Some of the ads are hand-painted, and the space feels open and makeshift, optimistic. On one side are stands and locker rooms. There is steam coming off the cool water. We slouch onto the deck. I spread my towel on the dew-damp concrete to stretch, holding the lying-down positions longer than necessary. The pool lights come up slowly. I roll off my track pants to apply sunscreen. My suit is still damp, raising goose bumps on my arms and thighs. Many of the other girls wear brightly colored tankinis bought for training camp; Lycra panels of purple, yellow, and orange, florals and wide stripes.

Warm-up is eight hundred meters swim, kick, pull, swim. We are given thirty seconds to get in the pool, by the hand of the pace clock. We either inch in, bouncing toward the deep end, or plunge and swim furiously to get warm. Within twenty seconds, everyone is in and under.

After warm-up I get out to use the bathroom. Walking back to the pool I stop short. The top of the wide staircase, leading to the deck, and the bottom of the bleachers frame a breaking tropical sunrise. I'm serenaded by sky blue and pink, an intense, Tahitian Treat pink. Popsicle, Care Bear, little-girl colors. I've never seen sky like this. It's optical glucose.

As we head into the main sets, the sun appears. By seven-thirty it is clear and the ads surrounding the pool are sharp. I see them when I breathe. *Milo*, pull, pull, *Colgate*, pull, pull, *Pepsi*, *Sudsil*, pull, pull, *Carnation*. Between sets some swimmers pat zinc on their noses. Training camp practices are difficult. Our coaches work us harder than at any other time of the year, and it's understood that the pain will be unrelenting for the duration of the week. When practice ends, nobody bothers to change: we pull on shirts and shorts over our suits and pile back into the minivans, limp with fatigue, but cheerful in anticipation of a few hours of bliss—sleep, food, dozing, beaching—until we have to go back to the pool at four-thirty.

The heat covers us like a blanket. At the hotel we drape our wet towels over the balcony railings to dry. The sun is higher still, and hotter; some of us shower, some sleep, some prepare breakfast. My roommate Rachel makes pancakes and—too hungry to wait—picks one up in her hand, pours syrup straight onto her palm, and eats the whole thing, laughing. By noon, most of us are down at the beach, spread out on towels suntanning, or splashing in the waves. Erin gets her hair braided, the ends beaded in red, green, and yellow. The sun burns her scalp bright red; the cornrows will remain for a month after her return to Toronto. We don't swim in the sea, we just stand in the waves, being pushed gently around by them. We form little groups in the shallows and talk, shoulders burning. A few of us try backflips, look at stuff through our goggles. Our scale shifts in the open water, we are smaller.

The team is going to a hotel restaurant at a nearby beach for dinner on New Year's Eve, but I somehow talk my roommates into having a fancy spaghetti dinner on our balcony, then meeting the rest of the group at the hotel for the countdown. Between workouts we get a lift to town and spend the afternoon going from store to store buying ingredients. After evening practice we cook through our fatigue: spaghetti with fresh tomato sauce, two loaves of garlic bread, and fried plantains. We spread our table with a white sheet, dress in our nicest clothes—white jean shorts and a new Lacoste shirt for Shelley, a polka-dot rayon sundress from Le Château for me, a strapless top and jeans for Rachel, an Ocean Pacific minidress for Erin—and light candles. As the other swimmers make their way to the restaurant, they see our flickering ground-level balcony and approach, impressed. We speak in English accents and shoo them away from our table. Danny grabs three pieces of garlic bread, blows out our tea lights, and runs off, stuffing bread into his mouth and whooping hysterically.

Kevin, whom Erin likes, opts to stay in his room and sleep through the night. When I hear this I suddenly like him too. After dinner, Erin asks me to go with her to his room and persuade him to come out, but he insists on staying in; he's already brushed his teeth. We leave him in bed. Erin is disappointed; she wanted to kiss him at midnight. As we close his door I glance back at his body under the flowered hotel coverlet, his greenish chlorine-bleached head of hair turned toward the wall. Kevin has a small, cruel mouth I like.

. . .

Twelve years later, I find myself feeling smaller in the sea again, when James takes me on a short vacation, our first together. I have no idea how to "vacation," how to lie on the beach and relax, wade into the waves holding hands, how to dress for dinner, swan around in a fluffy robe, book a massage. On our first day I retreat sulkily to the bedroom with a book of Alice Munro stories, irritated by the expectation that I'll enjoy things I've never enjoyed. It dawns on me that I am now the normal person in the next hotel, listening to Nirvana. When James gets back from a tennis lesson, I'm in a better mood.

Watching him in the waves, I realize he doesn't see life as rigor and deprivation. To him it's something to enjoy, where the focus is not on to how to win, but how to flourish—in both the literal and the superficial sense. I can understand flourishes, the conceptual, the rare, the inspired, and the fantastic. James introduces me to the idea of bathing.

SIZE

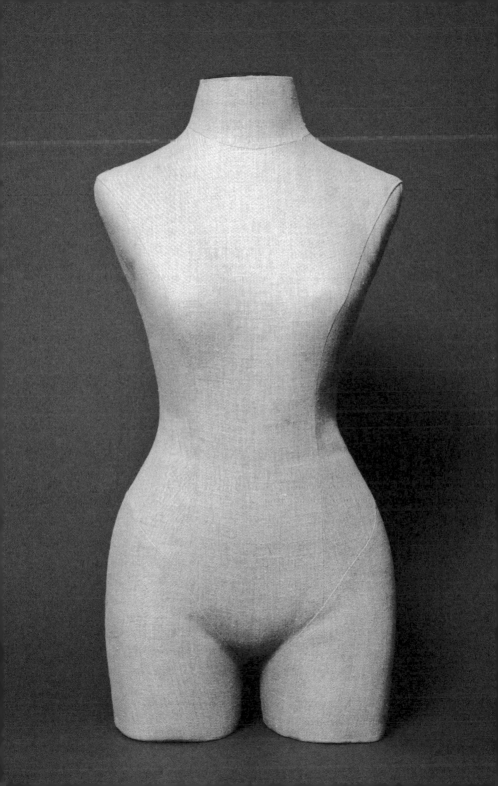

I am the first one in Stockholm's Centralbadet this Monday morning, followed by James, then by an old man wearing big yellow goggles, who does a steady breaststroke around the perimeter of the pool. Watching him, I switch to breaststroke myself and match his speed. It feels comfortable. It feels relaxing. As the three of us swim counterclockwise, I channel my old age, my flabby form, my unself-conscious senior. I think of the two older women I passed in the locker room, whose modest black tanks encased humps and bones and bumpy flesh. The cruel phrase a friend once used to describe a woman's backside: "a bagful of doorknobs." I watch my hands trace their double ellipse in front of me, my mother's wrists, my grandmother's knuckles.

1. Speedo black nylon, used as a doubling suit for training, 1988–1992.
We'd wear two, sometimes three suits to train in, the extra layers and weight providing drag. The suits were made of nylon, more durable and less flexible than Lycra. Some men's suits were built with mesh pockets that caught the water and billowed out in small cups at the hips. Before practice, we would keep our drag suits resting down around our hips. At a meet we'd roll them down wet after warm-up, as ballerinas roll legwarmers up over their knees and then down around their ankles. A black nylon suit would fade to a grayish-brown over time; a blue nylon suit to pinkish-gray.

1.

2.

The Centralbadet, built in 1909, is a gleaming wood-and-tile Art Nouveau pool. Its corners are round, and the surface of the water is almost two feet lower than the deck; I feel cupped, as if swimming in the hull of a ship. Behind curtains surrounding the pool sit wooden tubs, tanning beds, and darkened treatment rooms. One floor down, James and I find a large room of smaller pools, with a trough of hot water, and one of cold; a steep staircase that immerses the bather in waist-deep cold water; a deep hot tub shelved twice; and beyond that a large whirlpool with built-in recliners. The two older women join us in the hot tub, holding tightly to the handrails.

2. Speedo multicolored "paper suit," used for competition, 1992.
Called "paper suits" because their extremely fine-woven, crisp, paper-thin Lycra-nylon blend made a rustling tissue-paper sound when dry. We would order competition suits a few sizes too small, and wear them, beneath our clothes, pulled down around our waist or under our armpits before races. We were advised to splash water onto the fabric to ensure that the suit adhered to the skin and to prevent air pockets during the dive. The cut of the suits left most of the back exposed.

My Advanced Age Group coach Greg asked us one morning: What is the first thing we do, when we wake up for practice?

"Stretch," I said.

He shook his head no.

"Go pee?" someone else asked.

"Yes." Greg nodded. "And what I need you to do after you use the toilet is to weigh yourself, and write it down."

3. Speedo multicolored "paper suit," used for competition, Canadian Olympic swimming trials, 1992.

3.

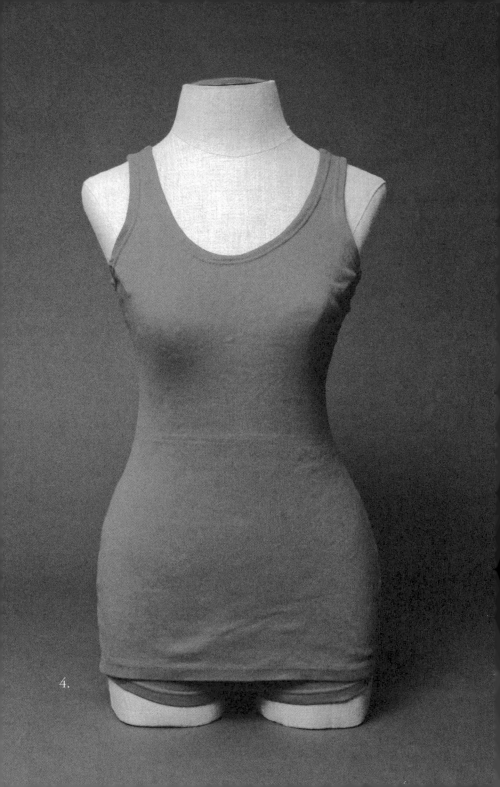

4.

After the finals at an out-of-town meet, the team would drive to a restaurant for dinner. In the bus on the way to the restaurant these were my thoughts:

Not nervous anymore.

Going to eat in a restaurant.

Can order whatever I want.

Tired and do not have to talk.

Hair wet clothes warm.

Will not have to clean up.

4. Vintage Aldrick & Aldrick red cotton suit, used for recreational swimming, 1998–present.

Purchased from Black Market Vintage Clothing, Toronto. Worn in rivers and lakes on a cross-Canada road trip; in Bobolink Pond, Ancram, New York; down waterslides at Camelbeach Waterpark, Pennsylvania; and in the Lake of Bays, Muskoka, Ontario. Also featured on the cover of *Saturday Night* magazine and in the *Süddeutsche Zeitung* magazine.

Dinners with the team look like this: Swimmers wear parkas or heavy coats, which, if they bother to take them off, are pushed inside out over the backs of their chairs. Hair is in various stages of damp. Boys' combed back, or sticking messily up. Girls' held in elastic bands, pulled into stubby ponytails. Prolonged exposure to chlorine makes hair stiff and dry, bleaching blond into stripes and green hues, brown into copper. The swimmers wear hooded sweatshirts, jeans or track pants, and have the red imprint of goggles around their eyes.

5. Vintage blue and white one-piece, no label, used for recreational swimming, 2000.
Stolen from Banff Upper Hot Springs, Banff, British Columbia.

5.

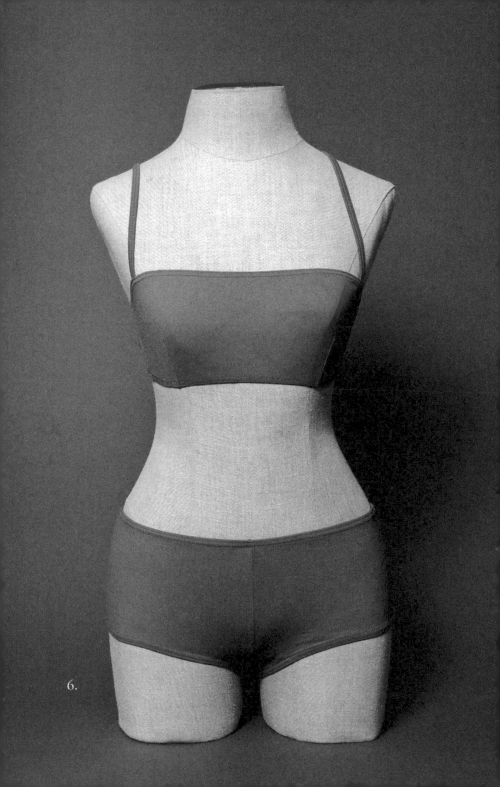

6.

The restaurant is a Denny's, a St Hubert, or a Swiss Chalet, usually near or attached to a hotel. We sit at banquettes or at square tables pushed together to accommodate us all. The waitress hands out laminated menus and pours ice water into foggy amber tumblers. When we order we ask for separate checks. Tips are left in change, in piles, once or twice beneath overturned sundae glasses.

6. A.P.C. red two-piece, used for recreational swimming, 2001–2008.

First two-piece purchase, made with Kim after a night of interpretive dance in an East Village apartment that Deirdre, who was breaking up with her boyfriend, was subletting from my new boyfriend's ex-girlfriend. Kim bought a brown version of the suit; we took the F train to Coney Island to see Peaches play the Siren Festival.

Being in a restaurant with my team is nothing like being in a restaurant with my family. With my family, I never order appetizers, rarely ask for sides, and the value deal is encouraged and often shared. But surrounded by my teammates, draped in happy fatigue and with cash in parka pocket, I order potato skins and onion rings, leave food on my plate, drink two root beers—and feel guilty afterward so do not consider dessert. The feeling of defying my parents is exhilarating and lonely. I don't see things the way they do, nor could I after crossing the appetizer horizon.

7. **Eres brown halter-neck bikini, used for recreational swimming, 2002–2008.** Purchased at Sunset Beach boutique, Shelter Island, New York. Worn learning to surf in Montauk, and swimming over the David Hockney mural on the bottom of the Hollywood Roosevelt Hotel pool with Jason, Gus, and Mike before our first book launch at Book Soup.

7.

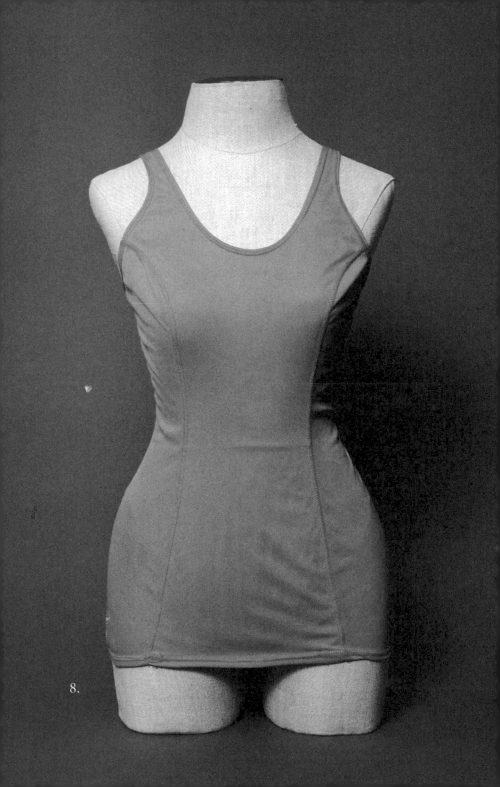
8.

I like to order something starchy, spaghetti with meatballs or two bagels with cream cheese. My first order of bagels with cream cheese is still vivid. The dining room was a bright glassed-in conservatory attached to a hotel, with a fountain and thick kelly-green carpet. The furniture was white wicker; the cushions were green-and-white gingham. The waitress brought me four stacked bagel halves, toasted an even, deep brown and lightly buttered. Alongside this came a glass dish piled with thick cream cheese. I slowly and steadily ate my way through the stack, staring at the gingham cushions.

8. Speedo red nylon suit, used for lap swimming at the West Side YMCA, New York City, 2002–2003.

Place of purchase unknown. The YMCA pool was a block away from the studio I shared with Paul. I did not have much work at that time, and at lunch I'd swim laps and then take my time in the steam room, staring at my knees.

I was thin, like my brother, and ate whatever was put in front of me. Until I was fifteen I was narrow, shapeless, androgynous. When I quit swimming in 1989, I ate erratically and experimented with anything that might offset the onset of late puberty and my habitual athlete's appetite. Before school I would go for a run with my dog, Rambo, then make two large peanut butter cookies in the toaster oven and eat them, steaming hot, on the bus. I learned how to bake bread and made a dense loaf every week.

9. Blue Lycra suit, no label, used for recreational swimming, Reykjavík, Iceland, 2003.

Purchased at the Laugardalslaug swimming pool. Jason and I went swimming daily when we were overseeing the printing of two books. It was April, cold, and the light fell strange and even. It was dark most of the time. We ate fruit and black bread with cheese in our room, and hot fish and vegetable dishes from the Oddi Printing Corp. cafeteria. I found a green army coat and a purple cashmere sweater in a thrift shop near the Sundlaug Vesturbæjar.

9.

10.

In the fall of 1991, I was swimming again and living in the basement of my brother's small East End Toronto house. Derek and three of his high school friends lived upstairs. I found two jobs: one, part-time, at an art bookstore, the other full-time at an art supply store, in the paper department. My manager there let me cut short my day by half an hour so that I could make my five p.m. practice at the pool. On my walk to work after morning practice I would buy a doughnut, or a package of two-day-old bran muffins from Rabba Fine Foods. I craved sugar.

10. Vintage high-neck psychedelic one-piece suit, no label, used for recreational swimming, 2003–2010.

Purchased from Black Market Vintage Clothing, Toronto. Worn in the Aegean Sea and in the Chateau Marmont swimming pool, Los Angeles.

I didn't know how to shop for food. My mother wrote out daily sample menus on pastel recipe cards, but I tucked them into my bookcase and bought bulky, instant things—baby carrots, peanut butter, bricks of cheap cheese. Sometimes I would buy a loaf of day-old raisin bread at Rabba, rip chunks off it for breakfast and lunch, and finally consume the last of it on the subway home after evening practice. At a routine weigh-in I clocked 134 pounds. My coach suggested I lose a little weight, and I realized that I was eating a loaf of bread a day. Embarrassed, I replaced the loaf with an apple and half a bagel, and dropped ten pounds in two weeks.

11. Calvin Klein black underwear set, used for recreational swimming, 2005–present.

Purchased at Laina Jane, New York City. Worn as a bikini more than as underwear.

11.

12.

As I lay in bed, alarm set for 4:15 a.m., I would hear my brother and his friends above my room, laughing and watching TV. At 4:30, after drinking a glass of milk, I would walk the six blocks to Danforth Avenue and take the Blue Night bus with the postal workers over the Bloor Street viaduct. I'd get off at Spadina, then walk south past the student housing and Chinese funeral parlor, to the pool. One morning I sliced my hand open while cutting a bagel, and Derek took me to the emergency room for stitches. As the doctor tugged on the frozen skin, I cried, my tears far out of proportion to the injury. He asked me what else was going on.

12. Vintage blue and white cut-out suit, no label, used for recreational swimming, 2005–2010.

Purchased on the street in the Essaouira medina, Morocco, June 2005. Worn to the beach despite the fact that my arms, face, and neck were covered with dark red hives and scaly patches. My skin was severely inflamed, the result of an attempt at homeopathy. James, Abdi, Chloe, and Paul did their best not to mention it.

Sometimes, mid-practice, students from the Sutherland-Chan massage clinic would set up their tables in a storage room off the deck. We'd be pushing through the main set when the assistant coach, Linda, like a fickle goddess, would pick five of us at a time to hop out. We'd spend ten happy minutes getting a rubdown from the massage students. The tables would be spread with dry white towels, we'd be covered in unscented cream, and our burning muscles would be kneaded into smooth, soft ropes. The students would remark how lucky they felt to be able to work on us, and we'd tell them they had no idea.

13. Vintage blue and white floral-printed cotton suit, no label, used for recreational swimming, 2006–2009.

Purchased at Portobello Market, London. Worn first in the infinity pool at Babington House, Somerset. James proposed in the pool. We swam around not knowing what to say to each other, went on a long bicycle ride, took pictures; then, later, in our small attic room, we fought and decided maybe marriage wasn't a good idea.

13.

14.

When Derek was working as a photographer's assistant, I'd sometimes meet him at the studio after practice, where his boss kept the lights low and the music melancholy and loud. Derek had joined a glamorous world of takeaway sushi, flash metering, and lab couriers. I would linger for hours, hoping to be given small tasks, while Derek made coffee with cinnamon in the grounds, the way his boss liked it. He showed me contact sheets under a loupe and Polaroids of dramatically lit Body Shop body wash. I'd sit on an apple box and look at *Vogue Italia*, *Harper's Bazaar*, and back issues of *Toronto Life Fashion* magazine.

14. Vintage Cole of California brown zebra-stripe tank, used for recreational swimming, 2007–2010.
Purchased at a tag sale in South Salem, New York, while Sara and Michael were visiting. Sara wasn't sure about the idea of wearing a stranger's used bathing suit. Slightly too short in the waist.

A thing I used to do when I was little:

I'd line up a handful of Honey Nut Cheerios in a row and eat them, one by one, in order of ugly to pretty. Finally there would be one left: the winner of the Honey Nut Cheerios beauty contest. I'd admire it—the winner was usually two stuck together with honey-nut coating, or one whose middle was filled in with a thin sugary pane. Then I'd eat it.

15. Rachel Comey, gray and black print two-piece, 2009.
Traded for designing prints for Rachel's Spring/Summer 2010 collection, not yet worn.

15.

16.

While in Stockholm, James and I ride bicycles to the Hallwyl Museum. Wilhemina von Hallwyl's Carrara marble bathroom displays the heat lamp she used daily for her bad back. A canvas strap that supported her head is still slung, striped and faded, across one end of her bathtub. Countess von Hallwyl and her husband, Walther, built and moved into the mansion at 4 Hamngatan in 1898. They lived there alone, their three daughters—Ebba the suffragette, Ellen the sculptor, and Irma the socialite—having grown up and moved out.

16. Speedo fuchsia and black tank, used for lap swimming at King Pool and at the Claremont Hotel & Spa, Berkeley, California, 2010.
Purchased at Berkeley Sports. There are two lap pools at the Claremont Hotel. When I visited, the more serious swimmers were using the colder, shorter pool, which was full and difficult to navigate. The deck was scattered with pull buoys, kickboards, flippers, and a prosthetic leg. The longer pool was warmer but nearly empty, so I finished my lengths there.

The countess's collection is extensive and endearing, a mix of the sentimental alongside the rare and valuable. Stacks of table linens; rows upon rows of uselessly small glasses, sorbet cups, toothbrushes, baby teeth, Chinese porcelain; a long attic room tiled with oils; gleaming swords and guns. I warm to the acquisitive countess, navigating the world as I do by my own love of things. I leave the armor room and take the first steps up a staircase as my headset intones: *"On the stairs ascending to the bedroom floor, the countess tragically fell to her death in 1930."* I think about something the psychologist Adam Phillips wrote: "Our excesses are the best clues we have to our own poverty; and our best way of concealing it from ourselves." I think of my own collections (old white trousers, hardcover books, striped towels, bathing suits, fake oranges) and wonder what my unknown deprivations are. I wonder, What, if I stop accumulating, will I confront?

17. **Coral and warm-gray tie-front reversible bikini, no label, used for recreational swimming, 2010.**
Purchased reluctantly at the Cotton House boutique, Mustique, after realizing I couldn't dive or jump without having any of the vintage suits I had packed slipping off. Least hideous thing in the shop.

17.

18.

We head out of Stockholm to Kolsva, where we find a *badplats*, a swimming area, on the Hedströmmen River. As we approach I see the broad, bare backside of a man toweling off, his skin glowing against the emerald green of the trees. A woman in a bikini sees us and motions to him. I look away and whisper, "Naked!" to James. The couple pull on clothes, and by the time we are dockside they are packing up and leaving. A family of five occupies the dock; the three blond children drop lily pads into the water and watch us as we wade in and swim, through water the color of breakfast tea, to a floating raft about fifteen meters away.

18. Lyell black smocked bathing suit, used for recreational swimming, 2010.
A birthday present from James, worn swimming with Jason in Tunkhannock Creek, Pennsylvania, after stopping at an antiques store, coming across a Ku Klux Klan robe for sale, and leaving as quickly as possible.

I remember seeing a dead body on the beach in Międzyzdroje, Poland. During the summer of 1993, Jason and I drove along the Baltic coast, sleeping in the car on beaches. We swam at sunset, and were wading aimlessly when we felt a gentle movement of people leaving the water. As we looked around, following, we saw the reason. In the fading light, the dark silhouette of a body covered in a blanket was laid on the sloping grade, its feet lapped by small waves.

19. Vintage Boutique Pia pink and purple two-piece, used for recreational swimming, 2010.
Purchased at Zachary's Smile, New York City. Worn for a quick swim with Kristin, Jay, Rachel, and James in the middle of the Black River crocodile safari, Jamaica.

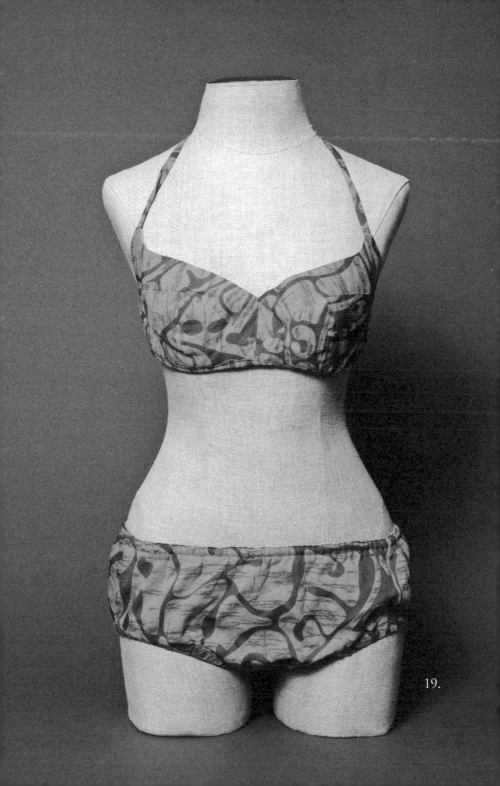

19.

20.

The women's swimming pavilion at Saltsjöbadens Friluftsbad, in the Stockholm archipelago, was built in 1913. It is a long U-shaped structure, directly on the shore. The two-story building is painted a pale sea-foam green and lined with tidy, white-doored wooden cabins and decking. It's a prettier version of the brown and blue men's pavilion standing across the family beach. I had read about the men's and women's swimming areas, but it didn't dawn on me until I got there that this separation involved nudity.

20. Arena Waternity teal tank, used for lap swimming, 2010.

Purchased at Paragon Sports, New York City. Worn to masters team workouts at Baruch College pool.

Beyond a small door (monitored and opened only long and wide enough to let one person pass) the sunny double deck of the Dambadet encloses a section of shoreline on three high sides. I look out over the bodies covering the planks. I have my Speedo in my bag, but hastily tally that only thirty percent of the women wear suits. I let myself into a nearby cabin and think: When in Sweden.

21. Speedo Fastskin LZR Racer Elite technical suit, used for competition, 2011.
My first technical suit. I do a test run in my backyard pool before using at a swim meet in Wilton, Connecticut. It makes me feel more buoyant, but also as if I've been swallowed by a boa constrictor.

21.

22.

As I walk, naked, along the wooden deck, among the tan, blonde Swedes reclining on their beach towels, I'm less self-conscious than I expected. Women glance, I glance back, but it feels like an internal shrug, a relief to be naked, outdoors, and feel so safe. In contrast to the chatter and shrieks of the family beach, the Dambadet is quiet. Most of the women are reading. I step down the wooden steps that lead into the water. It is cool, perfect hot-day temperature, tasting only mildly saline.

22. Anne Klein black tank, used for recreational swimming, 2011.
Purchased on Etsy, worn swimming in a backyard pool in Bellport, New York, but more frequently as underwear beneath semi-transparent dresses.

The water is a beautiful olive-green color, turning my skin ochre beneath the waves. I like seeing the body I usually see in a tub or shower out here, in the sun, in the sea; gliding naked around other women's thin bodies, fat bodies, saggy and taut parts. I feel good about my own—a relief after the habitual scrutiny of clothing myself—and at the same time feel invisible and unself-conscious. Out of the water my movements are still modest: I hold an arm between my breasts, I step around towels and legs with economy. But the feeling is very matter-of-fact, no need to yank Lycra over butt cheeks, no worrying about my bikini line, no anxiety over lane direction, speed, time.

23. Vintage Charmant mustard-yellow and white polka-dot bikini, used for recreational swimming, 2011.
Purchased at Gadabout, Toronto. Worn hosting a pool party where guests played Bananagrams, croquet, and Catchphrase.

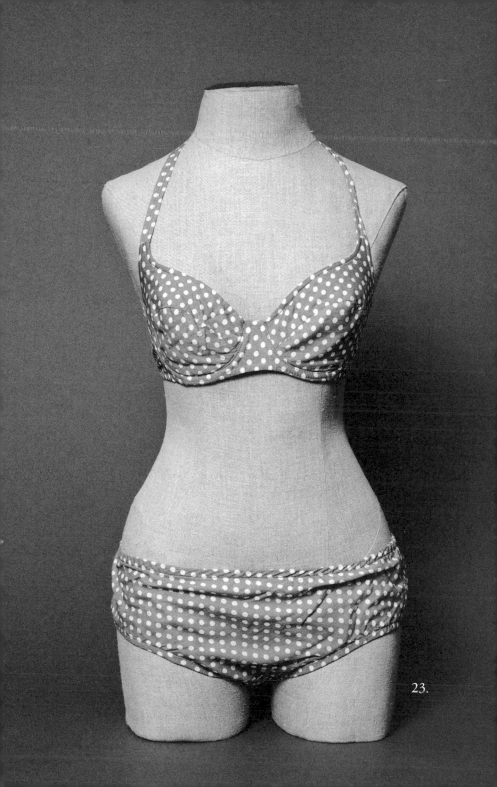

23.

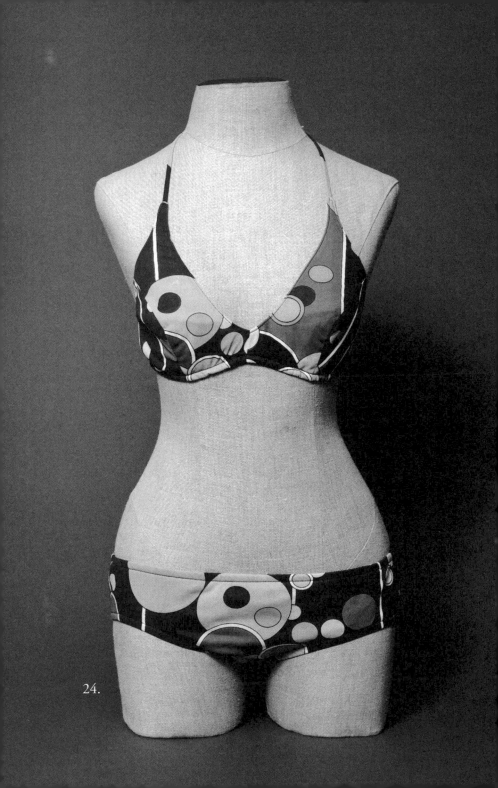

24.

An indifferent animality trumps anything erotic. As though in our polite blankness we are brushing up against one another, our furs, our similarities. I still see myself as a young swimmer, as a tube in a tank, as a neutral, androgynous athlete. But without my Speedo I am a bather, a body. As I approach forty, my swimmer self erodes with the onset of the gravity-bound realms of marriage and family. Swimming is my disembodied youth, yet I am rapidly becoming the embodied present.

24. Speedo multicolored nylon bikini, used for recreational swimming, 2011.
Purchased at Gadabout, Toronto. Worn in Vals, Switzerland, and Kolsva, Sweden. Bottom left behind at the Bains du Marais, Paris, but later rescued from the pocket of a robe, fished out of the bottom of a laundry bag.

A friend e-mails me a link to some photos he thinks I'll like. They are by George Silk, of fourteen-year-old diver Kathy Flicker in Princeton University's Dillon Pool in March 1962. The black-and-white images have a spirit-photography quality; the waterline displaces Flicker's head, and refracts her body, inflating its size nightmarishly. What falls below the water's surface is free of our usual grasp of physics. The pictures achieve something rarely articulated about the metaphysical state of swimming: The body, immersed, feels amplified, heavier and lighter at the same time. Weightless yet stronger.

25. Speedo black high-neck tank, used for lap swimming, 2011.
Purchased at Le Bon Marché, Paris. Found in a section on the third floor devoted to *le week-end*: expensive soft-shouldered cashmeres and cottons in muted, subtle colors that put me in mind of obscure minor royalty. Worn for lap swimming in the Piscine de Pontoise, where I forget to bring a towel, so *après* swim, I cycle-dry on my Vélib' city bike back to the hotel.

25.

26.

As I swim past a pair of older Swedish women talking to each other, heads up and paddling, a young woman jumps off the first level of the platform tower. I follow her pale form as she swims toward the steps, and I get out and head for the tower myself. A wooden spiral staircase leads to the two upper platforms, the top one forty feet or so above the water. The second platform is about twenty-five feet above the water, and it is this one I leap from, naked, into the green waves.

26. Aquarapid purple tank, bought in Turin, during the 2010 Artissima art fair, used for recreational swimming, 2010–2011.

Worn in a Holiday Inn pool, Minneapolis, before attending the opening of Jason's first solo museum show, at the Minneapolis Institute of Arts. Taped to a wall near the pool is a piece of paper that reads:

POOL NOTICE:

The black marks on the bottom of the pool were caused by a guest, who was an art student, and experimented with a waterproof marker. The pool is clean and safe. In order to remove the marks, we have to drain the pool. We have chosen to do that at a future slow period so that our guests now can enjoy the pool.
Thank you, Management.

ST. BARTS

St. Barts, the last day of December 2009. The sailboat is anchored offshore. It is four p.m., the sun is low, hot, egg-yolk yellow. Four of us—me, James, André, and Xin—decide to swim to the beach with flippers. I'm the strongest swimmer, James the weakest.

Being pool-trained, I'm used to seeing four sides and a bottom. When that clarity is removed I get nervous. I imagine things. Sharks, the slippery sides of large fish, shaggy pieces of sunken frigates, dark corroded iron, currents. I can swim along the shore, my usual stroke rolled and tipped by the waves, the ribbed sandy bottom wiggling beneath me, but eventually I get spooked by the open-ended horizon, the cloudy blue thought of that sheer drop—the continental shelf.

When I saw a cross section of the shelf in my fourth-grade geography textbook, I ran my finger from beach out to sea, imagining it was me and imagining the increasing depth beneath my kicking body, my suspension in it uncanny and diminishing. In lakes I think of the ancient tree trunks crisscrossing the bottom, black cities of wood rot and skeletal corridor. I imagine my foot brushing something, stirring up fibrous mud. The wreck of the *Edmund Fitzgerald.* The Loch Ness monster. I avoid being in the water next to the hull of a ship or the descending green post of a dock. Any unusual bulk in the water near me is mildly unbearable. If it is dark it is worse. Thrilling and dreadful.

James and I swam off a sailboat with André a few years before, in the Aegean. The boat had put down anchor in a small bay. The sun had set and the sky was navy. I was below deck, and heard a loud splash outside the cabin porthole. André called to the rest of us.

The water was black, but André's body was outlined against it in martian green. Phosphorus. I wanted badly to get in. From the ladder I leapt as far from the side as possible and began swimming around the boat. James came in after me and swam in the opposite direction, so I turned and swam toward him, not wanting to feel alone next to the dark hull. I wrapped my arms around his cool shoulders, scared and ecstatic. Swimming that night, through the phosphorus, with the stars and shredded pieces of cloud reflected in the surface of the glinting, living water, I felt suspended, tiny. On one side of me, the boat's tall prow swept darkly up out of the water; on the other, the anchor fell taut and deep. My perfect nightmare. I went once around the boat with James, then found the ladder and sat on its rungs, heart pounding. I splashed the glinting green water between my knees. It was my thirty-first birthday.

Looking across to the St. Barts shoreline, we pull on fins and begin the swim to land. I am quickly twenty meters away from James. André and Xin are ahead of me by ten. James does an easy breaststroke with his head held up. I swim back to him and suggest he do the crawl, but he doesn't answer me. I explain to him that fins help a flutter kick but hinder a whip kick. He doesn't answer me.

I feel my body acutely in the water. Once in, I like to swim until I feel the edges of my limbs and a familiar strain. I take twenty long, strong strokes and look back. I've passed André and Xin; James is now a paddling speck. I swim back to him. He complains that his flipper is cutting into his foot. Once more, I suggest a different kick. He tries for a while, then goes back to what he was doing. I swim out again, then back. André swims to me and asks if James is okay. I tell him James's fins are giving him trouble. André swims over and offers to trade flippers but James says no, thanks. I am aware of a current, weak and not helping us inshore.

We all swim at James's pace for a while, and then André

and Xin move away. I stay next to James as we lose sight of them. Resentment starts to build. We are swimming so slowly I'm cold in the water. His inefficient stroke is infuriating. I go back to my usual pace, then double back to keep him within my sight. I can't leave him behind. I think of the ring he gave me three days ago.

I can tell James is tiring. The closer we get to shore, the harder I want to swim. I suggest he roll onto his back and do a butterfly kick to relieve his foot, which works for a while, but his stroke is resistance rather than catch-and-flow. As I swim next to him, my voice is full of false patience. He snaps at me about his flipper. I glance at my ringless finger as I swim away from him, then back again. It was too loose, so I left it at home, worried about losing it in the sea.

We finally reach the curve of the beach basin, and the waves gather us into the rowboats and splashing teenagers. I can see rocks, fish, and the sandy bottom, and swim quickly into shore. On the beach we take off our fins and lie in the hot sand. James rubs at his blister. We do not talk. The swim has taken forty-five minutes. I walk along the beach alone, then return. André trades flippers with James, and the four of us set off to the boat. The swim out is easier, the sun in our eyes. I swim fast, tugging out the thresholds in my arms and the tops of my thighs. James is far behind, so I double back again. Then set back out. I do this until we near the boat.

As we swim up alongside it, three passengers from a nearby yacht skim out toward us on bright yellow Seabobs. One wears her sunglasses perched on her head. We tread water and shake hands, and they offer us a turn on their machines. At top speed, the Seabobs remind me of resistance training with surgical tubing. During practice we tied ourselves to one end of the pool and swam to the other side, making only inches of progress as the rubber tube was stretched thin. At the other side we'd hang on to the wall, then let go, yanked across the pool like a hooked fish, water banking, as we stroked with superhuman results, the water roaring past. Sometimes the perfect first lengths of a race felt that way, where strength was effortless, its long-stored hours finally gushing out painlessly. The Seabob is a luxury-toy version of this.

James paddles in and takes a turn on one. It makes him giddy too. As we laugh, our sailboat's tender sputters up with two new guests. One of them, seeing us bob and wave, pulls her dress over her head and swan dives topless into the water. Later, on deck, she discovers that only one of her diamond hoop earrings remains in her ear.

PISCINE OLYMPIQUE

I check into the Westin, at the corner of Saint-Antoine and Saint-Pierre. The hotel is tall and sleek, but the pool is tiny, more of a tank. Its one redeeming feature: a glass bottom that overlooks the entrance drive. I have a couple of hours before I'm due at a Montreal bookstore to talk about a new series of paintings, so I go for a swim. It's impossible to do laps. As I make short passes across the pool, I see hotel guests silently get in and out of taxis, uniformed porters opening and closing car doors. I hope they'll glance up and see me floating overhead, so I can wave, but nobody looks.

After the trials in 1992, I stop training, and miss the coverage of the Barcelona Olympics by taking a summer course at an art school in downtown Detroit. I stay in an apartment on campus, cover the walls in cartridge paper and draw large portraits of men from photographs in old *Vanity Fair* magazines. Robert Wilson's face covers one wall, Tom Stoppard's another. After a quiet week of rote life-drawing classes, calls to a not-really-boyfriend, and diary writing, my supply of spaghetti and Granny Smith apples has dwindled. I need to socialize.

I make some friends in the apartment building who persuade me to buy a pair of Rollerblades. They teach me how to blade during the empty early-morning hours. We drive over to Wayne State and park, put on an R.E.M. tape, open the car doors, and roll round and round the paved university campus, up and down deserted Woodward and East Kirby. When I talk about swimming, my new friends look at me blankly, so we talk about art.

In September, my deferral over, I head to McGill for freshman year, with Chris. We move into an apartment at 2100 Rue Lambert-Closse.

Halfway through the year, our roommates Amy and Lisa, who found the apartment, decide to turn a large closet into another bedroom and advertise for a "gay-friendly" roommate. Chris argues that this is discriminating against straight people. Amy and Lisa insist it means friendly, not gay. I suggest we all move somewhere nicer and cheaper. We see one apartment that I still think about: Recently vacated by a McGill professor, it had the winding halls, hardwood floors, and tall windows typical of Montreal. The rooms were lined with built-in wooden bookshelves, making the walls a foot thicker, floor to ceiling. I dreamt of filling the shelves with beloved books; I imagined that the insulated, focused qualities of the professor still infused the space; I felt that if I lived there I would be smarter.

We do not take the apartment. Sumaya—both friendly and gay—moves in and sleeps on a peach-colored duvet on the floor of the large closet. She leaves big pots of spicy dal caking on the stove. Each morning, while my roommates sleep, I silently maneuver my green mountain bike out of our hall, down the stairs, and into fresher air.

I bicycle from Lambert-Closse to the Cégep du Vieux-Montréal pool, for swim practice with the McGill team. The post-Olympics season is quiet, the gears slowly beginning on another four-year cycle. Earlier in the year I was in Montreal to compete at the 1992 Olympic trials, held at the Piscine Olympique.

I still have a memo Byron handed out in February 1992, a photocopy, on canary-yellow paper. He drew the Olympic rings on a flag upper right. The memo reads:

TORONTO SWIMMERS: OLYMPIC TRIALS
AND OLYMPIC GAMES HERE WE COME!!

Our twelve-month build up to this summer is in its final phase. We have been able to stay close to our original plan: aerobic base in the Summer; aerobic and major strength focus in the Fall; boost of aerobic over Christmas; reduction in strength training focus with increase in racing in the winter. The results indicate that we are right on track to begin the final phase: the increase in speed work leading to the Trials.

SO . . . . . . LET'S DO IT!!!

The plan is very simple. Hard Work. Lots of it. Total focus and total sacrifice. No excuses. You CAN do it.

The memo, along with others outlining training and meet schedules, is tucked into a red notebook. Another scrap of paper reads, in my own handwriting: *"Things that will help me achieve my goals: STRENGTH: weight training, knees/kick stuff; HEALTH: plenty of sleep, rest; INTENSITY: focused, practicing tired; WEIGHT: ideal 122."*

Throughout the notebook are lists of food consumed and my weight. On one page I've written the time I want for the long-course 100m breaststroke, 1:10:00, one hundred ten times. This faces lines about how much I hate certain teammates. The book is full of exhaustingly purple crush-pining; lists of art supplies and baking ingredients; notes concerning the rental of a studio space alongside plans to see live bands (Rollins Band, Luka Bloom, Cowboy Junkies) and independent movies (*Angel at My Table, Rosencrantz & Guildenstern Are Dead, Diva, Last Exit to Brooklyn*). Every few pages I exhort myself: *"Focus Focus Focus." "Just swim."*

I can't recall much of those Olympic trials, but from the final pages of the notebook I can piece together what happened:

Tuesday: After a morning workout in Toronto, left for Montreal. Got a quick massage at 8:45 a.m. and joined a team meeting at 9:20.

Wednesday: Shopped for groceries and watched heats. Did a light swim at 12:30 p.m., shaved down at the hotel; returned to the pool to watch finals.

Thursday: 200m breaststroke. Swam a disappointing 2:47:43 and finished thirty-fifth. (Four years earlier I had finished eleventh.)

Friday: Light swim during prelims and read magazines in the Parc Olympique. Found a four-leaf clover, which I pressed into the notebook. That night the team had dinner at Pacini.

Saturday: Light swim during prelims. Ate an orange. Went to the movies (*Lethal Weapon 3*). That night my teammate Marianne made the Olympic team in the 200m IM.

Sunday: 100m breaststroke. A disappointing 1:17:52, finishing thirty-sixth. (Four years earlier I'd finished thirteenth.)

By the end of Sunday night, the Olympic team had been selected. My teammates Marianne, Gary, and Marcel had made it; Beth, Kevin, and Mojca had not. Beth had missed the qualifying standard by a hundredth of a second. A hundredth. I remember her face, glazed, stoic, on the medal podium. It was like watching the bereaved. Kevin had made the Olympic qualifying time but finished third, and the team took only the top two.

I got dressed and caught a team van from the hotel to the subway, then the subway to a pub, where I ate french fries. I talked to a heartbroken Kevin, then danced with him to "Let It Be." Beth, Kevin, Andrew, and I took a cab back to the hotel, where Kevin was locked out of his room and came down to mine. We walked to a McDonald's. It was drizzling. In the window of Dunkin' Donuts we saw Gary and Mojca.

When I got back to my hotel room I sat in a chair, feet on the windowsill, and listened to "One" by U2 over and over again on my Walkman. I watched the sun come up and saw a teammate, carrying a blue backpack, walk across the hotel parking lot. He got into his car and drove away. I slept. When I woke I packed, taking the fruit and the peanut butter, leaving my roommate Shelley the granola bars.

Stuck to the last notebook page is a candy wrapper from the Bar-B Barn on Rue Guy. Pressed between two pages is a dried brown sprig of something that may have been a lilac.

That fall, back in Montreal, I don't plan to continue swimming, but after the McGill head coach woos me over a mushroom omelet, I join the team on the condition I make up my own practice schedule. I phone it in, but for the first time in my swimming career, for those few brief months, I enjoy it. I walk out midway through the freshman initiation ritual (twice around the McGill track with a marshmallow tucked under each armpit and between the knees, wearing suit, cap, goggles, and sneakers) with impunity. The team has access to a private gym, where I spend happy hours in the fragrant steam room after weight-training/music-video-watching sessions. At varsity meets I room with my friends Andrea—a 1988 Olympic medalist and 1992 Olympic team captain who bears her mind-blowing accomplishments lightly and has a whooping, filthy laugh—and Ojistoh, the team beauty, a Native Canadian medical student who eats baked beans straight from the can and cucumbers like bananas.

2100 Rue Lambert-Closse is a long, three-story brick building, with a flat white portico veined with cracks. Inside, the foyer and halls are painted a glossy, sickly lavender, and give off a warm cumin scent. Our apartment is narrow, high-ceilinged, with warped hardwood floors. My room is at the end of our hall, overlooking the front path. Chris has the room next door, where he reads *Details* magazine, listens to Soundgarden and Nirvana. He's starting to play music with his friend Vernon;

they are forming a band. Amy's boyfriend Dave teaches me some Fugazi chords on his guitar in the living room one night.

Vernon is visiting Chris when he inexplicably collapses outside 2100. I'm in Toronto when it happens, and stay there for the funeral, but when I come back to Montreal, I stand at my window looking down at the path, wondering at what Chris has gone through.

My McGill history of photography classes take place in a dark room. As the professor clicks through slide after slide, I'm stirred by the fine, pale faces in daguerreotypes; by William Henry Fox Talbot's grainy *nature morte* and Julia Margaret Cameron's images of girls and women, sepia profiles, thoughtful, strong. A hundred ghost stories, in black-and-white, flash up one by one out of the dark.

Hours between classes and workouts are spent in the McGill Library, where I look at publication design annuals from the 1970s and read about Pentagram and Push Pin Studios—a cool, candy-colored version of America, literate and illustrated.

These eight months are a hummus-and-steam-room-scented chrysalis—my age and my swimming age aligning. As if Montreal were an atoll enclosing the pools of Etobicoke and the open sea of New York. I swam easily—undermotivated, away from expectations, through dual meets with Dalhousie and Yale, Latin declensions, Fabien Baron–era *Harper's Bazaar*, Leonard Cohen's Gallic deadpan, and Paul Westerberg's shaggy yearning—toward the conclusion of my competitive swimming career.

Chris is still living in Montreal, with wife, baby, and Oscar-nominated production company, and he stands at the back of the bookstore during the event. Over a beer afterward, he describes cycling past Lambert-Closse, which was boarded up and condemned. He says it was as though it had been stopped in time, the precise moment we all vacated. Me to Brooklyn, Chris to the Plateau, Amy to Toronto, Lisa to Concordia. He says it was the opposite of seeing an old house occupied by a new family, full of unfamiliar details but still sweet, clean, and alive.

"So much happened there," I say.

"Yes, so much happened in that foyer." He nods and repeats: "So much happened in the foyer."

The bar is loud and I have not seen Chris in years and the woman sitting across the table from us changes the subject to Halloween costumes and then the other friend I am with wants to leave.

COACHES

I dream about swimming at least three nights a week. In these dreams there is always a race, and there is always someone watching, usually a man. I've sought out that figure—the coach—throughout my life. I always seem to have one, to find a version in the men I work with, my bosses; I always seem to rely on one to draw out my "How high?" best.

It would have begun with my father, a libertarian who tried to address normal childhood conflicts creatively. When I refused to eat beef tongue he used it as a lesson in trade—asking me, age six, what it was worth to me to not have to eat it. Desperate, I told him it was worth five dollars, my total savings from birthday and Christmas cards. He thought this was fair, and the exchange was made.

Though we attended Catholic school, my father insisted that my brother and I not be baptized until we were old enough to make the decision ourselves. Thus my feelings of fraud for at least seven of my eight years of formal Catholic education. I remember the principal of my school saying that only those who are baptized go to heaven; as for the others, "Good luck to them."

Less liberating was his attitude toward corporal punishment. At one point he thought making me and Derek sit in a horsehair chair in a corner of a dark basement for half an hour would be effective discipline for our childish crimes. When he realized this was only terrifying us, he stopped. He's been remorseful ever since, but I now can't sleep without a light on. As a result of these strategies, and the long letters he would write to me on the importance of honesty, of study, and of not smoking, I was reasonable. I learned to be good.

When I was twelve a coach remarked I had a "feel" for the water. After basking in the attention for a moment, I understood exactly what he meant. I still do. It's a knowledge of watery space, being able to sense exactly where my body is and what it's affecting, an animal empathy for contact with an element—the springing shudder a cat makes when you touch its back. When I'm dry I bump into things, stub toes, miss stairs. I prefer the horizontal, feet up, legs folded over armrests, head propped sideways on my elbow.

I don't understand how to really draw until a teacher says, "Imagine you are running your hand over the surface of what you are drawing."

A life-drawing class I take at Pratt Institute in 1993 includes a trip to Columbia medical school to sketch from cadavers. While a live model poses on a table, my instructor manipulates the body of a flayed, immaculately preserved cadaver in imitation. We are then invited to touch it. It occurs to me that even the most intimate relationship with another person can't allow this kind of investigation. My fingers hyperextend the knee and then slip behind the patella, following the muscles as they weave beautifully around each other. They're like silk cord and they smell like wet cardboard.

Down the hall is a dissection room. I somehow find myself there, alone, before the rest of the class arrives. Two tidy rows of yellow-tarpaulin-draped cadavers lie upon their stainless-steel tables like giant bananas. The wet-cardboard aroma is heavy in the air. I turn and stare at the sink while I wait for the others.

In the middle of the room is a vat full of heads, and another with a female study cadaver dissected so that, as with a pop-up book, we can open the rib cage and inspect the organs piece by piece. I rummage around in her abdomen and my instructor points out that the supple little coin purse I'm holding is a uterus. Later that night I have a craving for chicken.

When I was fourteen my father gave me a book called *Revealing Illustrations* that he had found at Crown Assets. It was about the work of James McMullan. I loved it, asked for a set of decent watercolors, and spent days copying the paintings onto pads of paper.

Bored at Pratt one night, I look up James McMullan in the Manhattan phone book. To my surprise there is a number, and an address on Park Avenue. I dial. A man answers. I ask him if he is the illustrator James McMullan and he says yes. Then I ask if I can show him my portfolio. He says he's in the middle of a move and suggests I call back in three weeks when he's settled.

Three weeks later McMullan's assistant shows me into a bright studio and motions to a wicker chair where I can wait for Jim to finish a phone call. I recognize the chair as one I painstakingly copied from a watercolor sketch in his book. (His sketch was swift, confident, exactly the mood of a beloved chair in sunlight. Mine looked like it was made of hairy crab's claws.)

When he gets off the phone, Jim flips through my portfolio and tells me that I do not know how to draw at all, that everything I have done is gimmick and style. He turns to me and asks bluntly, "What do you want?"

I ask him if he needs an intern.

I work for Jim Tuesdays and Thursdays. After three weeks of filing, sorting, cleaning, and research, I ask him to look at some new drawings. Some dispiriting sighing, some head shaking, and then he turns to me: "You have to WORK."

I sit in on two of Jim's classes at the School of Visual Arts. He teaches us how to draw, taking us through the experience of paying attention and focusing. It's like playing scales: we draw over and over, as honestly and clearly as possible. It calls up a memory from when I was seven: piano lessons in the basement of a music store in Mississauga. My piano instructor, a fat Italian man in a thick cardigan, falling asleep as I plunked on the keys. Waking only when I stopped, whereupon he'd say, "Re-pet-ah, re-pet-ah." I'd leave the lesson, mimicking him while I kicked the gravel and waited for my mother's car.

After my internship with Jim, there follow more internships, I find more coaches to look up to, who impart varying degrees of influence and wisdom. I get my first illustration assignments from *The New York Times* and *The Globe and Mail*, an art internship at *Harper's Magazine*, then a real job, at a Canadian newspaper, the *National Post*, editing and designing a culture section, then art directing its weekend magazine, *Saturday Night*. When the magazine is canceled in 2001, I leave for London, where I spend a strange winter and spring in love with two men, drawing furiously. I finally return to Toronto when the severance pay ends and my application for a U.S. green card comes through. I have no work, no money, two failed relationships, and a diagnosis of chronic depression.

I don't remember those bleak months, just my brother coming over to my apartment and sitting in my bedroom while I cry; my parents' concern, confusion, and support; my friend Sara's infinite patience with my ruminative, annoying phone calls; the little blue pills and the little pinkish-brown ones. I start cognitive behavioral therapy but I can't imagine feeling better. In my doctor's office I hold up a worksheet and ask him how many I have to fill out before I feel better. He says a hundred. I get it, like laps. I can do a hundred. I settle in, blinker myself, count the laps. Six months and a hundred fifty worksheets later I feel better. The drugs help me focus, and I finish a series of drawings, self-publish them in a book, move to New York with the green card.

One day, while James and I are watching Roger Federer play tennis on TV, the commentator—filling the silence between serves—blandly repeats the well-known fact that Federer does not have a coach.

I sigh. I think: I don't need any more coaches.

"I don't need any more coaches," I say to James.

He glances at me. "You don't need any more coaches."

James is the opposite of a coach. He encourages me to sleep in, isn't bothered when I cancel, shrugs at my whims, my mistakes, my detours into self-indulgence. I tell him about Edmund Wilson, who would shut his then wife, Mary McCarthy, in a room for hours under orders to write a story. I tell him I find this romantic.

"I don't have to shut you up in a room," James says. "You do that yourself."

One night, I e-mail my father to ask him about Studebakers. He replies, with embedded snapshots of his cars. One includes him and my mother in the snow; another is of me and Derek with our first coach.

Hey Dad, I have a few questions for you:

1. Were you the president of the Ontario Chapter of the Studebaker Drivers Club?

No, never was president, just an ordinary member.

2. Was the Hawk a 1964 Gran Turismo?

Yes the white 'supercharged' Hawk was a '64, the first Hawk I owned was a '62 Gran Turismo and there were several others in between.

Summer '73

3. Was the Loewy Avanti a 1963?

Yes, 1963 supercharged Avanti. Loewy took credit but the designer most responsible was actually Bob Andrews, employed by Loewy.

4. Was the Champion a 1953?

Yes 1953 Champion Coupe.

And what is the area between the backseat and the bottom of the back window called? Where you'd put mothballs?

In those days, and still today, it was known as the 'parcel shelf'.

Luvya! Dad

PRACTICE

One of Jim McMullan's favorite artists is Lucian Freud. In a short film about Freud by Tim Meara, titled *Small Gestures in Bare Rooms*, Francis Wyndham—whom Freud painted reading from a collection of Gustave Flaubert's letters—recites, in voice-over, passages from letters that he and Meara felt resonated with Freud's practice. Writing to George Sand in 1875, Flaubert asserts that the artist should appear in his work no more than God does in nature: "The man is nothing, the work is everything." Wyndham then quotes from two letters written by Flaubert to the poet Louise Colet in 1853: "I think that the greatest characteristic of genius is, above all, energy. . . . What seems to me the highest and most difficult achievement of art is not to make us laugh or cry, or to raise our lust or our anger, but to do as nature does, that is, fill us with wonderment. The most beautiful works have indeed this quality, they are serene in aspect. Incomprehensible."

When I hear this I think of athletes.

At the end of *Michael Phelps: Inside Story of the Beijing Games*, a documentary about Phelps's eight-medal Olympic sweep, are three bonus chapters. They are called "Michael on Herman the Dog," "Michael on How He Likes Texting," and "Michael on How Much He Eats." In the footage—contrasting dramatically from the races and studio analysis—Phelps, in his sweats and bare feet, reclines on his sofa and scratches his bulldog, Herman. He explains that when he's not swimming or sleeping, he's hanging out with Herman on the couch, texting, or playing video games. His voice is deep, nasal, and relaxed. His dog snores and shuffles around, blinking sluggishly: a perfect anthropomorphic of the off-duty swimmer. Phelps on Herman: "He's pretty chill, he's pretty low-key, as you can tell. He doesn't really like to move much, doesn't like to run around a lot. Every now and then he'll get a good burst of energy and runs around for a few minutes and he's done." Phelps plops Herman on the kitchen floor and reaches for a box of cereal.

Serene in aspect, incomprehensible.

I had a brief encounter with Lucian Freud. I was visiting London with James, early in our relationship. At dinner with two friends, I recognized a solitary man at the bar as Freud. Knowing I was a fan, one friend urged me to go speak to him, and I approached. He wore a scarf, and his pale skin and features were delicate. His eyes were very clear and blue. I told him how happy his work made me; he thanked me and invited me to sit. After offering me one, he smoked a cigarette. We each had a glass of fino. We spoke a little about the restaurant and the food. I had my sketchbook with me and showed him some drawings I had recently made. He described them as vigorous and asked if I painted. When I told him I didn't much, he talked about his process, said that when he painted, he did not make drawings. He then recommended a Frank Auerbach exhibition and asked me how long I would be staying in London. When I mentioned the name of my hotel, he told me he swam in the pool there regularly, especially in good weather when the roof opened to the sky. His dinner arrived and I said good night. In the back of my sketchbook he wrote his address, and the address of where he breakfasted each morning.

When I got back to the table, everyone was finishing dessert. My food sat as I had left it, half messed with and cold. I had been at the bar for three-quarters of an hour. My friends made little of it, but in the cab, James was brittle with anger. We fought in our hotel room. At four a.m., unable to sleep, I took the elevator down to the business center in my pajamas and robe, and wrote James a letter of apology.

. . .

One night, Jim McMullan invites James and me to the opening of a show of his poster work for Lincoln Center. The gallery is full of people, and Jim's posters line the walls: *Carousel, South Pacific, Six Degrees of Separation, Arcadia, Ah, Wilderness!* I can hear Jim intoning the titles of these plays—he has a dramatic, passionate way of speaking, and I have never heard him mumble. Everything about him has intent. As I wander around the room and look in the vitrines that display his studies and notes, I remember my drawing classes with him. How painful and frustrating they were. I glance toward two tables piled with crudités, cheese, and tortellini on sticks. Some of Jim's students are hanging out near them. I feel something like jealousy.

The arrangements of Jim's multiple sketches illuminate his practice, how he pushes past perfect moments of clarity to get something even better. His rigor is astonishing. My own sketches betray distraction and cross-fingered stabs. Spaghetti on a wall. Jim once generously described my work as "blithe."

The idea of specialness occurs to me one night when I can't sleep (or bake). That as good athletes, we defined ourselves as special, then submitted to a routine in which we did exactly as we were told. I think of the limitations that "specialness" requires: doing a series of very unspecial things, very well, over and over, a million times over, so that one special thing might happen, *maybe*, much later. So—I think to myself in the four a.m. blear, face squashed into my pillow—specialness is sanctioned, rigorous unspecialness. An unexpected feeling of relief flows over me. Then dissipates as I start grinding my teeth.

During the last third of *The Magic Mountain*, I start to think about how the body bestows specialness in prowess and illness. Both involve enduring some kind of pain. When Hans Castorp's uncle flees Berghof Sanatorium, escaping the calm smug of the ill, the *unspotless*, Mann (or his translator at least) describes his afflicted nephew's attitude as "callous" a number of times. I recognize the description—and the feeling of superiority the "special" have toward those they consider "un"—but also, a callus, a hardened patch of skin formed by repetitive motion. Does specialness beget callousness, or does the mind conjure specialness? Does the mind follow the matter of the body into specialness? What separates rigor and brilliance?

While watching the French Open one morning on television, I leave my chair and walk toward the kitchen. John McEnroe is commentating, and as I put the kettle on I hear him mention that Rafael Nadal is playing through a sprained ankle. I remember the blunt fact that when I was training, I was in constant pain. Not just the sharp pain in my knees, which was taken seriously, but a dull, steady pain in my arms, back, shoulders. Pain when I sat down, pain when I got up, pain when I leaned back in a chair, pain when I reached for the salt or sharpened a pencil. Thinking of stoic Nadal, I remember how I ignored, then eventually forgot about, pain when I raced, and even to some degree during practice. It was as though pain on land was there to remind me to get back in the water, where, after a certain threshold, the pain went away. For an athlete pain is not a deterrent, because the only place the pain will be eclipsed is in practice or in competition.

Watching some hip-hop dancers on TV, a friend asks me: "Why is it so fun and satisfying to see a group of people do exactly the same thing?" I think about this—how we apprehend the life of the special body, choreographed movement, dance, planes flying in formation. It *is* satisfying, but also like watching something defy gravity, or more specifically, defy the wilderness of our bodies in time. All that work and then, finally, something levitates. When the minute stresses of practice fade, the specialness emerges. There is a quotation from *On Directing Film* by David Mamet that I underlined in 1993 and have never forgotten: "Stanislavsky wrote that the difficult will become easy and the easy habitual, so that the habitual may become beautiful."

Glenn Gould, explaining his love of the recording studio, described it as "an environment where the magnetic compulsion of time is suspended—well, warped at the very least. It's a vacuum, in a sense, a place where one can properly feel that the most horrendously constricting force of nature— the inexorable linearity of time—has been, to a remarkable extent, circumvented."

It's appealing to think in compressions of time, a month of Sundays, four seasons in a day; this might be why stitching and knitting metaphors complement the idea of time so well, something understood best through relative degrees of distance. The Olympics are often described as four years in two weeks. There is the popular phrase "An athlete dies twice."

This idea of dodging time reminds me of a *Muppet Show* segment that still moves Derek and me. It is a rendition of Jim Croce's "Time in a Bottle": An elderly scientist Muppet wanders around his cluttered laboratory singing the song as he mixes powders and potions in test tubes. He gulps his concoctions as others bubble over on burners, and verse by verse he grows younger, his halo of white hair turning gray, his dome covered again in tufts of red, his gravelly tenor growing clearer and climbing higher. Finally, with one last reddish drink, he explodes, returning to his true, eldest age, and gazes at his lab table hopelessly.

Artistic discipline and athletic discipline are kissing cousins, they require the same thing, an unspecial practice: tedious and pitch-black invisible, private as guts, but always sacred. One night, over a second round of Bloody Marys at Fanelli's, I ask a few of my friends what they hate but force themselves to do. Bikram yoga. Child care. Work. Swim practice. We bang on the table. We firmly agree that one really ought to do something one would prefer not to do.

Whenever I begin a large project, and when, as a swimmer, I contemplate a practice, a mental image appears: a grayish Sisyphean mound I need to ignore in order to begin to climb. After twenty years I still search for the dumb focus I had as a competitive swimmer. After a hundred workouts I might be faster. After a hundred CBT sheets I might feel better. After a hundred lengths I might be healthier. After a hundred pages, a hundred sketchbooks, when will it feel right?

My fingers used to be pruney, from being in water. Now they're ink-stained. I replace my laps with stacks of sketches, and my teenage dread of workout with my adult dread of bad work. I fill sketchbooks with repetitive studies, happy only when the last page is finished and I can look back, pick out the handful of good pieces. I paint series after series: my dog, the trees in my yard, all of the glasses in the house; flowers, Parisian signage, hardcover books, leaves, movie stills, a reservoir view, a single pitcher, patterns, photographs of people playing charades.

During a cocktail party in a London home, I stop in front of a small charcoal drawing of a swimming pool teeming with bodies, by Leon Kossoff. It is noisy, exciting, and alive. Kossoff, in a rare 2007 interview, age eighty, said of his practice: "Every day I start, I think, Today I might teach myself to draw. . . . It doesn't make any difference how long you do it, it's always starting again, one's always got to start again."

When I read in an obituary that Cy Twombly's father was a prominent swim coach, I start to see Twombly's paintings as thrashing laps, as polygraphs, as pulse rate. I wonder if I'm drawn to his work because he might have had an athletic habit he metabolized then rejected.

During my first year in New York, I see Ellsworth Kelly's *Dark Blue Curve* at the Guggenheim. I keep going back to it, in books and online.

The first piece of art I bought was a small watercolor by Marcel Dzama. In it, a woman in a blue dress and blue boots is suspended beneath a few feet of water. Her back arches, feet sink, arms are flung above her head. Small bubbles rise to the surface, where choppy waves peak.

In my studio, I work beneath a David Hockney poster for the 1972 Munich Olympics. A drawing of a diver, the pool water in wobbly grid, sunlit in shades of aquamarine and white.

Every day I walk past an old oil painting in my hallway. I found it in a junk shop, a moody view of Poolvash Bay in the Irish Sea, seen from Balladoole, a Viking burial ground.

In my office, tucked behind a framed photograph of James, age twenty-four, rowing a boat in Central Park, I have a postcard from Ryan McGinley's series of Olympic swimmers, originally commissioned by *The New York Times Magazine*. It is of Natalie Coughlin, mid-crawl, fingers splayed, grasping at the water in front of her. It reminds me of how, though swimmers spend hours catching and cupping water in the most efficient way possible, their hands are always relaxed, in a sensitive yet decisive rock-climber hold, where the water can be caught and passed.

Next to my bed I keep a framed anonymous black-and-white snapshot of a woman in a bathing cap, swimming in open water. Her body has reached the most extended part of the breaststroke and she glides away from the photographer, the dark water ruffling around her. The photographer watches her swimming away; she is perfectly framed, maybe unaware that her picture's being taken. It reminds me of the love I have for James when he doesn't know I'm looking at him.

I've dragged a tiny jpeg of a watercolor by Laura Knight, titled *Girl Bathing*, onto my computer desktop. I've seen it only in this low-resolution version: a woman in a purple bathing costume, removing a shoe before swimming. I like postures like this—inward, small moments of body maintenance— bathers; Bonnard's hypochondriac wife in the tub; variations on Fedele, "The Faithful One," a Greco-Roman sculpture of a boy who, after delivering a message, stops to remove a thorn from his foot.

I first saw a slide of the sculpture in my tenth-grade art history class. I remember being touched by the story of duty over pain. It's a pose that we all feel to look at, the strain in our hips and spine as we draw our foot up and examine our sole.

MOM

There is a British expression that James likes to say in exaggerated mockney: *Who's he when he's at home?* It refers to getting above oneself or one's station. It could be a Canadian thing too, this taking someone down a peg, like the title of the Alice Munro collection *Who Do You Think You Are?*

One day, while my mother is visiting me in New York, I take her to Barneys to use a $400 store credit from a returned wedding gift. I want to restage our shopping excursions to Mississauga malls and flea markets, I want to buy her something luxurious, beautiful, something irrational and ridiculously priced.

We start at the basement level, cosmetics and perfume, where we try to find a stick of her favorite foundation.

We approach one counter. The saleswoman swipes at my mother's cheekbone with various flesh tones. I notice a fly on my mother's coat shoulder and brush it away. As the sales-woman checks the stockroom for the correct shade, we wander among the displays, glancing at lipsticks and scented candles. My mother walks with her hands held behind her back. The saleswoman returns empty-handed and tries to convince my mother that her skin is actually a different shade, one cor-responding to something they have in stock, but my mother won't have any of it. I proudly steer her to another counter. Here a cheerful man sits her down and makes her up, applying foundation to one cheek in a pinkish shade, the other in a more olive tone. He also applies undereye concealer, blush, and lipstick. My mother looks at her face in a mirror, chooses the pinkish foundation, and declines my offer to buy her the concealer, blush, and lipstick.

We escalate to accessories, on the main floor. My mother admires a few things. She tries on a mink headband, a cash-mere snood, a pair of fur-lined gloves, but after glancing at the tags shakes her head no. I suggest that she think in terms of something she likes, not something she can afford. She shrugs, eyes darting from Italian sock to mitten to handbag. We head upstairs to the first floor of designer collections. She runs her fingers over the pieces that catch her eye, turns over the tags and whispers prices, incredulous, under her breath. On the next floor I ask her if she sees anything she likes. "I'll know it when I see it," she says. She touches the shoulders in the rows of soft knits and smooth cottons. On another escalator I pluck a price tag out of her hair that must have been attached to the mink headband: $675. My own eyes widen.

Looking at the shoes, she marvels at a towering turquoise pair, clownish and exaggerated. I encourage her to try on some simple Chanel flats like the pair of mine she has borrowed for the day. She looks at the price. "No, no, they're not nice."

On another floor I show her some of my favorite designers. Some imaginative knits, some clever design details, some beautiful pajamas. She looks, glances at tags, drops her hands.

I find myself getting impatient. I remind her that she can pick out anything she likes, that we have $400 that has basically grown on a tree to put toward it. As her eyes glide appreciatively over the mannequins' clothes, she denies wanting anything.

On the top floor I suggest we buy the rest of the makeup she tried on, but she suddenly admits she saw a gray sweater she liked; she does not remember where. We head down floor by floor, searching for the gray sweater, inspecting corners we missed, touching and smoothing sleeves. It reminds me of visiting a furrier's with my mother and Derek, I might have been eight. While she consulted on her layaway fur, Derek and I ran through the sleeves and skirts of squirrel, raccoon, and mink, rolling our eyes, stroking the empty arms, and cooing, "Softeee tofteee . . ." over and over again. I hid in the middle of the circular racks, feeling the fur on my face.

We still haven't located the sweater by the time we reach the ground floor. My mother looks around at the hats and gloves as though she's lost something. It is a state of confusion and mild panic I recognize; I've felt it too. It's about looking for something you don't naturally want, for fear of missing out on what you think you do. Taken on, it's a heavy, absurd confusion—the feeling of not knowing yourself.

There's something "Rocking-Horse Winner" about the moment: the dark places where shame will take you and exhaust you. My seeping impatience is tempered with remorse at bringing her here, the extravagance of Barneys, thirty years after Dixie Value Mall. Why should I expect her to be seduced by things I myself am uneasy about? I want to get out of the store, but I suggest we retrace our steps upstairs.

On the top floor she considers an iPad case, a purse. We have been in the store for close to two hours. I suggest a simple bag, a scarf, a wallet. No. No, no. She fingers a different cashmere cardigan and I urge her to try it on. A salesgirl, wearing the same cardigan, retrieves her size. I look at my mother in the sweater; it is nice, but trendily cut. The arms look strange.

She prevaricates, finally decides against it. On the fourth floor she stops short in front of a row of knitwear and pulls out the gray sweater. It is $900. I pause. We both laugh. We take the elevator back down to cosmetics, find a gardenia perfume she likes, buy the concealer, the blush, the lipstick.

TITANIC

My first visit to Ottawa was with my sixth-grade class, touring the oak-paneled, green-carpeted chambers and hallways of the Parliament buildings and peering into the store windows on Sparks Street. Later, I swam in meets at the Nepean Sportsplex, and stayed with my team at the Embassy motor hotel, where one night my roommates and I snuck out and walked aimlessly along the highway for two miles, giddy with our jailbreak, looking for a gas station with vending machines so we could buy junk food.

The next series of Ottawa visits revolve around a friendship. Adam and I are roommates first, a couple briefly, then quarrelsome but loving friends. His influence gives me a taste for the unapparent, nuanced qualities of things. He lends me Celan, Baudrillard, Beckett, makes me tapes of Ol' Dirty Bastard and Aphex Twin, teaches me how to cook and taste good food. With him I begin to look at art and people with equal affection and appreciation. I begin to understand the value of contradiction and the fun of false notes.

I meet Adam's family in Ottawa and visit their cottage on Meech Lake. Years later I read part of *The Magic Mountain* aloud to him in hospital, then, arriving a couple of hours too late, see his body at the Élisabeth Bruyère palliative care facility. I fly back for his funeral a week later.

After the ceremony, a group of Adam's friends and family gather at Meech Lake, drink red wine and talk about him. The lake is frozen. Nine of us put on our parkas and boots and set off across it with Maya the Weimaraner, and Ivana, Adam's collie mix. The night is cold, moonless, and black, and some of us carry our glasses of wine, which we sip, fingers freezing, as we follow the ribbing of snowmobile tracks. The flash of my camera lights our progress now and then, leaving glowing negative shapes of each other in our vision. We walk side by side, without seeing one another's faces, wiped out by grief, glad to be together. Looking at the photographs from that night you'd think we were celebrating a birthday; we look tired, but in all of them we're smiling.

Adam's mother tells me there is a famous pool at the Château Laurier, the hotel where I am staying. Before I check out, I take the elevator down and look at the pool from the gallery, wishing I had packed my bathing suit.

My most recent trip to Ottawa is to attend my cousin's wedding and launch a posthumous collection of Adam's short stories. James and I book into the Château Laurier. Our room is not ready when we arrive, so we go for a swim while we wait. The Art Deco lap pool at the Château was built in 1929, and the basement complex was billed—in the mustache-twirling language of the time—as "The Hydro and Electro Therapeutic Department Turkish Baths and Swimming Pool of the Château Laurier, Ottawa, Canada." Photographs in the reception area show men in unitards leaning on machines that look like giant megaphones. A woman lies on a pristine bed, eyes covered by goggles. An androgynous head, wrapped in a turban, pokes out of a large iron tank. In a photograph of the pool, one side is flanked by cane lounge chairs upholstered in palm-tree-patterned fabric, spotlit by seven enormous heat lamps. The Department offered guests treatments for rickets, infantile paralysis, and tuberculosis with quartz ray heaters, autocondensation cushions, carbolic acid baths, and ultra-violet rays.

I give the attendant our room number and take a towel. The ladies' locker room is two flights down. It is a brightly lit warren—short hallways of white-painted wooden cubicles, each with a bench, hook, and mirror. The showers are dark-tiled, smelling of perm solution. The locker room is empty and silent but for the thin hum of the lights. I change in a cubicle, leaving the door ajar, and hear someone enter and turn on a shower. As I pass the anteroom that leads to the shower stalls I immediately think: ghost.

On deck, the pool is all slabs of amber and green marble, surrounded by fish-, shell-, font-, and wave-themed ironwork. Overhead, twenty-four globe lights are suspended from propeller-shaped ceiling fixtures. The deck slopes slightly toward two heavy columns at the deep end, the grotty tiles auguring verruca. It could be Lex Luthor's subterranean residence. Along one deck I recognize the same seven heat lamps from the photograph, now weakly illuminating cheap plastic pool furniture. At the shallow end, a marble enclosure that used to showcase a fountain stands empty.

As James sidestrokes and I kick, we talk about the backyard pool of his childhood home, where he learned to swim. He describes his near-drowning: His mother and sister had gone to change, leaving him behind on the deck. When he reached for something in the water, he slipped into the deep end. He clearly remembers thinking that since he didn't know how to swim, if he sank to the bottom he could walk up to the shallow end and get out. His next memory was of waking in his bedroom, covered by a blanket with an electric heater trained on him full blast. His sister had jumped into the pool and yanked him to the surface, and his mother had lifted him out. I try to imagine a world without James. Then think about Adam. A melancholy wave washes over me as I buss the water with my lips. I watch my progress against the side of the pool, where red and black tiles tidily spell out: | STEPS 7 1/2 FEET DEEP | + | | + | 9FT. DEEP | + | | + | | + | | + | 5 FT DEEP | + | | + | | + | | + | 3 1/2 FT DEEP STEPS |

I shower and change. As we leave, we pass a tall framed rendering of a steamer, black smoke billowing from its stacks, passengers waving from the deck, its wake swamping a small sailboat off its starboard prow. A handful of seagulls glide beneath the simple white letters spelling T I T A N I C. Next to that image is an equally large one of a stern, bearded Charles Melville Hays. Between the two frames is a small plaque that reads:

Charles Melville Hays, general manager of the Grand Trunk Railway (1896), perished on the ill-fated Titanic when returning from England. Hays was the inspiration behind building the magnificent Château Laurier.

. . .

This is the second time the *Titanic* bears down on me in a pool. In London a few months earlier, I visit the swimming pool available to guests of Durrants Hotel, at the Fitness First health club, Baker Street.

Health club locker rooms are waltzes of averted gaze. I wish I could stare at people getting changed; I'm convinced all other women know something I don't—about grooming, about their bodies, about things I never learned to do because I was too busy swimming. But I face the lockers, strip under my shirt, pull my suit up under my towel.

In my periphery I notice a lot of black. Black tights, black heels, glossy black ponytails. It is a little before nine a.m. and I've collided with the post-workout pre-work crowd, dressing for the office. The air smells great. After an "All Swimmers Must Shower Before Entering Pool" sprinkle, I survey the deck. It's a small pool, twenty meters long. Ellipticals and treadmills are parked behind the glass windows at either end, their passengers' blank, determined faces staring out over the water. I find a lane to myself, slip in, and start swimming. The water is too warm, so I think of the opposite—cold water.

The day before, I took the Jubilee line to the O_2 bubble in Greenwich to see *Titanic: The Artefact Exhibition*. The disaster interests me from a swimming perspective; Alcatraz does in the same way. The thought of swimming to freedom in shark-infested waters; the thought of swimming away from a massive, sinking ship in the dead of night in the frozen Atlantic—I dread these unfathomable situations yet relish imagining them. When I was fourteen, a Filipino aunt living in San Francisco heard of my love of swimming and sent me a pink and black *Alcatraz Swim Team* sweatshirt. I wore it until the lettering faded.

At the entrance to the exhibition I am given a boarding card bearing the name of a real *Titanic* passenger. The man explains that at the end of the tour I can check to see if I survived or not. I look at my card: Berthe Antonine Mayné, a twenty-four-year-old cabaret singer traveling first-class en route to Montreal. She was the mistress of Quigg Baxter, also twenty-four, a Canadian hockey coach who had dropped out of McGill University. He bought her the ticket and booked her passage under the alias Madame de Villiers.

The tour starts with the ship's bronze lookout bell and proceeds through first class to second, third, boiler room, and bridge. Along the way we are presented artifacts recovered from the *Titanic*'s debris field: a bow tie, a full bottle of Champagne, a new pair of socks, gratin dishes. The exhibition is moving, though overproduced. The sounds of heaving iron ship are piped into the sets; in the boiler room we hear hissing and clanging. But the artifacts at the center of the show manage to find their emotional bull's-eye, and the unpredictable, normal lives of the passengers and crew emerge. In the final room a plexiglass case encloses a piece of the ship's iron hull, from C deck. The sign reads: "Touch the *Titanic*." A hole of about one and a half inches is cut through the top of the plexi so a visitor can extend a finger down toward the scrap and, indeed, touch the *Titanic*. I look at the small grubby cloud on the black metal where people have stabbed their fingers. It's a strange, morbid glory hole, a Blarney stone of tragedy; me, the doubting-Thomas tourist. There is something Egyptian, a telescoping of fate and time and the grave, about the moment, something that makes me hesitate before I touch it. But then I do: I stick my index finger through the hole and touch the *Titanic*. It is cold.

At Fitness First, I do only sixty laps, eager to get out of the close basement air. In the locker room a woman beside me pulls on a black pencil skirt and black silk shirt. Her black patent peep-toe pumps have little black bows.

"She cut her head open on the kitchen table," she explains to another woman. "They might have to restitch her if she opens it up again."

I realize she is talking about a toddler.

"Where did you get that shirt? It's nice," her friend asks.

"This? It's maternity. I just tuck it in. . . ."

I walk past a line of women blow-drying their hair and watch them while I spin-dry my suit. They are glossy-lipped, clean, and office-ready. I am wearing a ripped vintage dress over my pajama bottoms, feet shoved into men's paddock boots. I don't have a brush. I feel sloppy and wonder for a second if they might think I am a resourceful homeless person using the showers. I remember the office job I left a year ago, where I was part of a good team. Much as when I swam, I'd get home exhausted at eight p.m. and stare like a reptile at a plate of food.

I look in the mirror at my reflection, the red goggle marks around my eyes. I cover my wet hair with a hat, leave.

Our room at the Château Laurier is still not ready, so we head to the bar for some lunch. We are seated next to a player piano that churns out Joplin and Mozart. James points out the damper pedals that move by themselves. "Phantom pianist," he says. The Château is a little spooky. Its wide arched halls are similar to those in Kubrick's Overlook. The elevators make wailing noises as they ascend; the beveled leaded windows, turrets, and heavy oak doors telegraph a dramatic sense of what goes unseen, of privacy and transience. I buy a copy of *Haunted Ottawa* and read that the fifth floor—the one we are staying on—is rumored to be visited by the ghost of Charles Melville Hays, who might sing in a stairwell and brush up against women while they shower. The opening of the Château was scheduled for April 26, 1912, but because of the *Titanic* disaster was delayed until June 1.

When I get home from Ottawa, I google Berthe and Quigg. She survived the sinking, he did not. Then I do an image search for "pool on the *Titanic*." I find a few renderings and images labeled "pool like the one on the *Titanic*," some images of the pool on the *Olympic*, the *Titanic*'s sister ship, and one that claims to be the pool on the *Titanic*. It's a black-and-white image of a tanklike room, walls and ceiling of girded iron. A row of what look like changing cubicles can be seen along the left wall. A staircase leads into the pool, down which a blurry figure descends. At the top of the staircase another figure stands and watches. A small clock high on the wall is the only decorative touch. One round life preserver hangs on a rail along the right side of the pool.

GOGGLES

In 1984, when Derek and I first joined a summer swimming program, we became obsessed with goggles. My hero was the Canadian champion Anne Ottenbrite—a blonde breaststroker who wore a pair of wide, round Speedos. I wanted a pair of those goggles. When I finally got them I thought I looked faster.

At the 1984 Olympics in Los Angeles, Ottenbrite won gold in the 200m breaststroke and silver in the 100m wearing the Speedo goggles. But Victor Davis won gold in the 200m breaststroke and silver in the 100m in a pair of squarish Arenas, with black lenses and opaque white sides. Alex Baumann won the 200m and 400m IM in Arenas. By the end of the summer, I switched to a pair of squarish black Arenas that I regularly rinsed out with tap water as the instructions advised.

By 1988, when I was swimming seriously, minimal Swedish goggles had arrived in southern Ontario. These were molded plastic eyepieces that fit securely into the eye socket, without any rubber or foam lining the rims. At the 1988 Olympics in Seoul, Janet Evans won her 400m and 800m freestyle and 400m IM gold medals in a green pair. There was a coach who sold Swedish goggles poolside at Ontario meets for $12. I bought two, a red pair and a brown pair that came, unassembled, in narrow ziplock bags. Brown for training, red for racing. These goggles marked a step up in my swimming career, from okay to good. It was the beginning of my loyalty to equipment, to rituals and patterns. These goggles are a Masonic handshake. Even now, if I see other swimmers using them, I know they know.

Since I quit competitive swimming in 1992, my exercise routines have been a combination of jogging, kickboxing (briefly), swimming laps at the Y, swimming laps in my backyard, swimming laps with a group of Italian illustrators before heading to a juice bar where they smoke and drink carrot juice, tennis lessons, yoga, an early-morning boot camp, and, after being persuaded by a guard or coach on deck who notices my stroke, tagging along for various masters team swim workouts in different cities. When I do this, it starts out great, but I eventually grow shy of the mid-set banter, get discouraged by my practice times and uncomfortable with my loss of autonomy.

When I decide to push past these issues and join a New York masters swim team, I take the training back up like an old habit, an outgrown winter coat or friendship. It's familiar territory, but, as a teammate points out, I need a pull buoy and flippers, and it's the perfect excuse to look for new goggles.

Flicking through the selection at Paragon Sports, I see they have a few based on the Swedish design: foamless, socket-fitted molded plastic goggles that you assemble yourself. One version is called the Socket Rocket.

The night before a morning workout I find it hard to contemplate getting up to swim. My head is full of protest, a persuasive voice tells me not to bother. I have to mentally freeze-dry these impulses so that my body gets up, pulls my suit on, ties my shoelaces, picks up my bag, and calls the elevator. From there—like getting into the chilly Hampstead pond—it is one fluid motion: street, blocks uptown, building, stairwell, pool deck.

Once I am on deck, my will slumps again and the petulance seeps in. For the first hundred meters the water feels resentfully cold. In the face of the oncoming meters and the interval training, the inner whining becomes a wail. I blur my already blurry vision, and force my body to eat the meters, eat the laps. My body is constantly in motion, while my brain is glued to the clock, willing the minute hand to move, to eat the minutes. My head and my arms are like a bickering couple, beseeching each other to *chill*.

I clearly have not Made a Commitment, defined in a 1987 memo that my coach Greg made, xeroxed from the book *The Nuts and Bolts of Psychology for Swimmers* by Dr. Keith Bell. I still have it. The spread he copied includes two paragraphs titled "Make a Commitment."

> A commitment is important. Once you have set a long-term goal, you have decided to make the trip. Without a commitment, however, you are liable to question each step of the way.
>
> Commit yourself to an intense training program. Don't allow yourself to be making decisions about whether to attend a given day's practice or whether to cruise through the upcoming set. It doesn't make much sense to have to decide whether to take each individual step in a trip you have already decided to make.

Do I have a long-term goal? If anything, it's to figure out what to do with something I do well but no longer have any use for.

The one thing that I am formally trained at is swimming.

I'm aware I rely on this training when I'm working, that I know when to push through and when to rest, that I've figured out the equivalent of drills, interval training, and performance when I'm on deadline or trying to realize a project. But I don't know where to put the old skill, if I can, or even want to, incorporate it into my adult life.

Watching the even strokes of my masters teammates, I wonder whether they question what they're doing as much as I do. I'm used to hearing artists and writers question what they do; self-loathing, doubt, and mental blocks are par for the course. Athletes may wince at muscle pain but generally don't articulate their struggles. We respect them because they suck it up. They just do it.

My masters team holds practices at the Baruch College pool, in the basement of the Athletics and Recreation Complex, on the corner of Twenty-fourth Street and Lexington Avenue in Manhattan. In the bluish six a.m. light, the bronze life-scale statue of a smiling Bernard Baruch sitting on a bench in the lobby never fails to startle me.

Our coach is from Russia. He gives us textured workouts, often involving dolphin dives, fins, partners, and streamlining drills. He demonstrates each drill balletically himself from the deck, sweeping his arms around his body.

I like his workouts, and as much as my mind questions the point, my body knows exactly what to do, with some advanced level of competence, even grace. When I arrived for my first practice with the team, two other swimmers were stretching against the cinder-block walls and I joined them. The coach then led us jogging through the corridors and empty rooms of the basement. We ran up and down the stairs and did push-ups on pleather benches in an anteroom. While we did ankle stretches, the coach looked at my flexible feet and remarked: "You have been a swimmer all your life."

As the weather warms up, my focus weakens. I don't prioritize practices, barely manage one a week, dreading it in the days before. The usual frustration sets in when I can't make pace times. I'm embarrassed that the coach thinks I'm better than I actually am, and baffled when I hear another swimmer in the locker room after practice enthuse about what a kickass workout we just swam. The kickass workout only makes me grumpy. Where are my endorphins? I leave, sore, and think: You can't choose what you are good at, but does that mean you should do it? It occurs to me that I might be happier doing something I'm not good at. I have a bad attitude. I've noticed one swimmer who cuts corners and leaves early. I dislike him immediately, the way you dislike someone who reminds you of yourself. I think about quitting. But a team e-mail announces a local meet, and I decide to enter.

The day before the meet, when I tell James I have to carbo-load, he prepares sausage orecchiette with fresh chard from our garden. After dinner, in bed, I assemble a new pair of pink Swedish goggles I ordered online. On race day, I buy macaroni and cheese from the gourmet shop around the corner, happy to continue my carbohydrate binge. When I was fourteen, I'd cover a plate of my mother's spaghetti and meatballs with foil the night before a race. I'd then eat it, cold, for breakfast on race day. Tucking into my elbow pasta and Gruyère, at noon, alone in my apartment, I feel silly and have a pang of longing for the world I knew instinctively, the one I started eating spaghetti in. I see the rounded edges of my parents' kitchen countertop— a small swelling lip dropping to a ninety-degree vertical, ivory laminate chosen from a fan of colors on a beaded chain. The three steps leading down to our side door. The way the light from our basement window fell on a small snowdrift. The pale blue shade of the seat belt in my mother's station wagon.

The meet begins at three p.m., with warm-up at two. On my walk to the pool I buy a bottle of blue Gatorade.

On deck, Ludacris is playing over the loudspeakers, and the volume rises as I get in to warm up. I feel a little tired but good. I loosen up my arms and legs, try a few starts to make sure my goggles stay on, and do two sprints before getting out. The heat sheets are taped to the wall. I'm swimming four events: 50m freestyle, 50m breaststroke, 100m breaststroke, and 100m freestyle. No sign of my coach, or anyone I recognize. I seem to be the only person representing my team, so I sit against a wall between two other teams and watch the rest of warm-up, soothed by the beautiful strokes of some swimmers, the jerky awkwardness of others.

Watching a good swimmer is the visual equivalent of patting a dog's smooth head—something naturally, wondrously sweet and perfect. You can never tell if swimmers are good or not by looking at them on land. I watch one woman, tall and graceful, perfectly proportioned in her tank, get in and demonstrate a gruesomely mincing, hesitant freestyle. A short, chubby man, wearing no cap or goggles, dives in and executes a delicately churned butterfly down the pool.

It's funny that here—amid all this exposed adult flesh—I am my least self-conscious. Maybe my goggles and cap confer a sort of *Maskenfreiheit*. Without fashion, without slimming blacks and elongating verticals, there is less information to parse and judge, more to accept. Here my mind is the plus one. I don't wish I had a book or magazine to pass the hours. I watch the races, I sit silently, the most relaxed I've been in a long time.

The Bearcats, the team hosting the meet, occupy a single set of bleachers. The rest of the teams are grouped along the opposite wall. Keeping an eye out for my coach, I watch women with big wet circles on the seat of their track pants, men pale and hairy, coaches holding heat sheets, busy officials in shorts. One competitor's mother and girlfriend sit patiently at the end of my bench. I glance at the clock and think of this scene in cross section, happening four stories below street level, a pool full of busy adults, kicking and gliding and splashing on a Saturday afternoon. Overhearing bits of conversation I realize many of the swimmers also do triathlons. I can't even imagine. During the national anthem, a few swimmers place wet hands over wet breasts. I think of the traffic lights above us, the cashiers at the Duane Reade where I bought my Gatorade, who were short of change. I head for the women's locker room. It's empty, with a large shallow puddle in front of the sinks. It feels different from how it does during practice, like an elementary school lit at night, full of fizzy anticipation.

My first race, 50m free, is relatively painless; I win my heat, and then the event in my age group. Still no coach. I wait for my second swim, watching the heats, shifting on my wet bottom, itchy as the Lycra dries. (My brother called sufferers of this common swim-meet affliction the IBC: Itchy Bum Club.) I am irked in my second event, the 50m breast, by a woman in the lane next to mine, who finishes almost a second faster. She is wearing a technical suit I thought was prohibited. I look up her name and age on the heat sheets: she's ten years younger than I am. I vow to beat her in the 100m. There is a break at five o'clock, and I use the telephone in the lifeguard office to call James, who is in a car on the way to the airport. There are two pizzas reserved for the officials on the desk in front of me. I am getting hungry. Back in my corner the man sitting next to me opens a bag of peanut M&M's.

The 100m breaststroke is next, and staring at the swimmers in a state of strange hypnotism, I nearly miss my heat. The start, four lengths, and finish unspool like the poems I memorized in high school and remember slightly off: Magee, *sunward I climb / towards the tumbling mirth*; Housman, *Rose-lipt maidens sleeping / in fields where roses fade*. I know the pattern and the color, but I don't know the right words. I win my heat, beating the woman as planned. My time, which places me first in the country in my age group, is shockingly slow to me. *I shall wear my trousers rolled.*

One more race and I can go home. As I wait and watch the heats before mine, I remember how much I loved to race. My last event is the 100m free. The four lengths feel good, and so does the familiar push into the bank of pain and fatigue during the last two laps. I finish and glance at the board: 1:11:00. As I'm detangling my hair in the locker room, I realize that is the time I was obsessed with all those years ago for the 100m breaststroke, my microwave time. When I look up the results the next day, I realize I must have read someone else's time; mine is recorded as 1:10:51. The time places me third in the country in my age group. The rankings mean a lot and very little, like I did it in spite of myself. My body gets it more than my mind will ever appreciate. I give it that.

Body: "Awesome, right?"

Mind: ". . ."

Body: "I'm hungry."

I believed, for a while, in the aphrodisiacal qualities of my swimming. Sometimes, doing laps somewhere, I'd think: If only *he* could see me swim, he'd fall in love. It's like my karaokelomania: the belief that I wield a seductive wand and appear totally awesome when I'm up there singing Radiohead. Sometimes I have swimalomania.

While I'm voguing, in cap and goggles, in the back of my mind, I mention to James that there's a meet not far from where we live, in an outdoor pool. I think: He'll love me even more if he sees me race, he'll fall in love with me all over again.

He agrees to come watch me swim.

The meet takes place in a six-lane fifty-meter pool. It's surrounded by a low chain-link fence, and overlooks a small artificial lake. The meet day is sunny, an ideal outdoor-swim-meet day, the deck full of people, elderly, middle-aged, a few in their twenties. Some wear technical suits, most don't.

Swimming long course again feels luxurious, Californian. An outdoor fifty-meter expanse of water shimmers with the same kind of American dream that football fields and baseball diamonds do. Lines are crisp and colors are primary: swimming-pool blue, touchpad yellow, striped lane ropes, red and yellow flags. The pool, built in 1993, shows a little of its age, making it even more charmingly East Coast. It has heavy revolving doors leading to the locker rooms, old maroon starting blocks, and worn concrete decking. As I warm up, the bleachers begin to fill. I'm not feeling tip-top. My arms are heavy and my body drags a bit. I do a few starts and a few sprints, then get out and head for where James is sitting with my things, sipping an iced coffee. He's trying to read the paper over someone's shoulder as I approach.

The officials are having trouble with the touchpad system and ask the crowd for timers. James volunteers. I am the only swimmer in my age group again, and during my first race I swim beside a man in the thirty-nine-to-forty-four age group. I lead the field, but fade in the last fifteen meters and finish second behind my neighbor. I look at James and he gives me a shrug. I realize he doesn't get the whole age-group thing; to him a race is a race. Fortunately I win the heats of my next two races, giving the appearance of really winning. James offers a thumbs-up.

As I stand behind the blocks for my last race, an older woman walks past in her black and neon-green tank, two children in tow. "Mommy's about to race, honey."

It dawns on me why I am the only one in my age group. All the other thirty-five-to-thirty-nine-year-old women are pregnant, breastfeeding, or chasing toddlers. I cross my arms over my chest. I think the old thought: I have to start thinking about babies. Then: What do I think of babies? I think of being warned about performance-enhancing drugs twenty years ago and being encouraged to take them now. Of ovarian dysfunction at eighteen and now, at thirty-eight. How my body understands time better than my mind does. Then I think: This will be my final meet.

When we leave the pool, James strolls toward the car like a man who has just sat through an interesting lecture and is now peckish. There are no cartoon hearts popping out of his eyes, just a distracted practicality. On the drive home, fishing for compliments, I remark that I'm surprised my times were that fast, considering I hadn't really been practicing and I felt so crummy in warm-up. "Well," James says absentmindedly, glancing in the side mirror, "I overheard someone in the stands say they wondered if the pool was short."

I stare hard out the window. James notices.

"What? Sweetheart . . . was that a big contest?"

A contest. I stifle a smile out the window and my pride thins. It won't matter to James if I'm fast or not, a good swimmer or not. It's the last thing he'll be impressed by.

PIÑA COLADA

Nina and I sit under a beach umbrella, two piña coladas in. I've just finished describing to her how easily I develop crushes, using as an example the man in the waiting area at the airport who boarded the small plane after us and who, before takeoff, declined my offer of an organic macaroon, explaining that he did not eat sugar. I am extolling the virtues of such crushes, that women need muses too, need to get a little carried away by the physical, the way men always have been, that though you have no idea who these people are, do not act, and will never see them again, there are those thrilling minutes when you know your body with every cell and yet don't know yourself, when you imagine the people in your life don't matter and you would give everything up. Nina barely noticed the man, while I was gulping reality down with my bottled water, afraid to turn around, fearful that James, two seats away and three years into our relationship, could tell.

As I tell Nina that I am certain I will never see this man again, I turn to the water, glance up the beach, and suffer the stab particular to seeing a person you are not prepared to see. He is approaching an umbrella as an older couple, unmistakably his parents, make their way toward him from the water.

"Oh my God."

"What?"

"He's there."

Nina laughs a piña-colada-scented laugh.

He is tall, thin, smiling into the sun behind dark glasses. Seeing him with his parents is weirdly touching. He looks seventeen.

I whisper to Nina, "How old do you think he is?"

"I can't tell from here. Let's go swimming."

As we pass I hear him speaking authoritative German into his cell phone. I wave a friendly hand, as does he. He looks my age.

In the water I show off. I demonstrate my smoothest stroking, my most otterlike flips and dives. Nina swims over to some rocks and I do a few exhibition laps along the shore. I see him get up and walk out onto the jetty. He is alone. I swim away from him, willing myself not to swim in his direction, wishing I did not want to as much as I do, astonished at how much I want to see him in the water. I kick farther away and, treading water, watch him swim jerkily around the jetty and then get out.

Nina is back beneath our umbrella. I swim to the jetty and climb out of the water. I put my goggles beside me as I lie in the sun for a moment, and think about the bathing suit I am wearing (1970s vintage brown zebra-stripe tank, found at a yard sale in South Salem, New York). I have to pass the man and his parents on my way to our umbrella.

I am halfway down the beach when I realize I've left my goggles behind. Ten feet from their umbrella I stop, turn around, and go to collect my goggles. As I pass again, the man's mother steps toward me. I worry that she intuits my inappropriate crush on her son and now she is going to tell me to step off, but she doesn't. She makes friendly conversation and I immediately like her. We part, and I wave at the man and his father.

Back at our umbrella my heart is pounding. I sit and slurp the warm remains of colada in the bottom of my plastic cup.

Nina turns to me:

"Well!"

JAWS

*Quint: Y'all know me. Know how I earn
a livin'. I'll catch this bird for ya, but it
ain't gonna be easy. . . . Bad fish. It's not
like going down to pond chasin' bluegills
or tommy cods. This shark—swallow
ya whole. L'il shakin', l'il tenderizin',
down ya go.*

—PETER BENCHLEY AND

CARL GOTTLIEB, *JAWS* (1975)

*The swimmer must be afforded
advantages that only the pool can give;
a course of known length, smooth clear
water and well-defined lines on the
bottom of the pool, ending in distinct
cross-markings that indicate the
approach of the turning end, as well as
distinct markings on the end of the pool.*

—ROBERT J. H. KIPHUTH,

SWIMMING (1942)

The hotel is on the shores of the Bråviken, a handsome Baltic bay in Sweden. In the late-summer afternoon, its dock, a long T shape nudged by motorboats, beckons. We spread our towels on the planks and recline to warm in the sun. The water is green-gray; a strong breeze furrows the surface. James gets in first, and the waves take him quickly down-dock. Looping back, he swims out to one of six bright red buoys running parallel to the dock. He weaves in and out of them, then stops at one, tipping it toward himself to hook his arms over its mast. I watch him from my towel, dry and warm in the sun. As he swims around the tall buoys, I contemplate my aversion to open water. I wonder: How many competitive swimmers like swimming in open water? I compare my comfort in swimming pools to my discomfort in open water and my contentedness with solitude to my anxieties in close company. I think about limits, how easy life can be when it's limited, how manageable. Limits appeal to my controlling nature.

I ask other former competitive swimmers about open water, and most feel the same way. My former coach Byron does. His first objection is to the cold, his second to having to look to see where he's going, and his third he describes as the "What the hell is down there?" factor. He tells me about holding an ocean swim at training camp in Barbados, where one of his swimmers from Newfoundland refused to venture more than ten meters from shore for fear of sharks.

. . .

I watch James a while longer, then decide to get in. The water is warmer than the Vättern, a crystal-clear lake we swam in after breakfast. It tastes like diluted saltwater, with something green and mineral in the mix—thin chicken stock from a stainless-steel bowl. I swim toward James, who has let go of the buoy and now circles it. His scale next to the buoy makes me think of the scene at the beginning of *Jaws*, where a girl treading water is yanked sharply down, then flung violently through the dark water by something gripping her from below. She manages to grab hold of a buoy that clangs as it tips toward her, and prays aloud before being carried off and down. (Derek and I used to reenact this scene in various public pools when we were bored with Shipwreck.)

Feeling the brackish water shift between icy in one spot and warm in another, I imagine some kind of Swedish megalodon, algae-flecked and prehistoric, that's swum freakishly up into the bay. I head back to the ladder, get out, wrap myself in my towel and continue watching James swim among the six tall buoys. He looks happy.

Earlier, driving along the E4 past pretty countryside, I bickered with James about our evening plans and let fly a deep insult, engineered to hurt. Later, as we lay, peevish, next to each other on the hotel bed in our shoes, he whispered back what I'd said. I'd been awful. I'd yanked him down below the surface into my mean, cold dark.

Jaws, the movie, is about a man-eating monster. *Jaws*, the novel, is about marriage. The shark is a metaphor for infidelity, in the shape of Matt Hooper, a wealthy, scallop-eating oceanographer. As the great white glides predatorily along the shoreline looking for food, the oceanographer seduces Chief Brody's wife. Peter Benchley describes the (somehow more sordid) act of Ellen Brody's shaking bath powder into the cups of her bra and her pumps before he details their tryst: a sloshy lunch followed by sex in a motel room. Then he describes how Ellen remembers the scene:

> It was a vision of Hooper, eyes wide and staring— but unseeing—at the wall as he approached climax. The eyes seemed to bulge until, just before release, Ellen had feared they might pop out of their sockets. Hooper's teeth were clenched, and he ground them the way people do during sleep. . . . Even after his obvious, violent climax, Hooper's countenance had not changed. His teeth were still clenched, his eyes still fixed on the wall, and he continued to pump madly.

Jaws, the movie, is one of my favorites. As always, Spielberg casts the spell of suburban American life perfectly. I like his dining scenes in particular: Richard Dreyfuss as Roy Neary, mounding his mashed potatoes in *Close Encounters of the Third Kind*; then as Matt Hooper, helping himself greedily to the wine and Brody's leftovers in *Jaws*; Elliott ordering pizza; E.T. spilling milk. Spielberg's messy tables and twilit kitchen counters are the stomachs of his players externalized; they expose our own appetites for safety and familial security. Seeing his characters eating anticipates the inevitability of something consuming them.

While Spielberg's *Jaws* is Man versus Beast—not a love interest in sight (the pretty girl gets gobbled five minutes in)—Benchley's is about Man versus Sexy Beast. In the book, the shark threatens the prosaic town the way infidelity threatens our tidily framed ideas of marriage. It is part of nature, it is painful, it is down there.

One day I watch, in succession, *Deep Blue Sea*, *Open Water*, *Open Water 2*, and *Shark Week*, Season 6. It is a saltwater orchestra of cautionary tales: Don't genetically engineer sharks, don't trust a laid-back dive-boat crew, don't try to cure people's phobias, don't grab a cell phone from someone in the water, don't try to get a knife off a lunatic, and don't lie about your wealth. There are a few nice moments: the romantic frisson between two shark scientists; a married couple on a groggy hotel-room mosquito hunt; a husband and wife teaming up against an evil ex. Scenes of marital love seem to set up shark attacks particularly well.

Benchley based *Jaws* on the theory of the rogue shark—a shark that seeks out humans over its natural food sources—which has since been widely disproved. His novel and his shark loom so large in our imagination because we're invited to sweep our own dark tendencies under the shark's great white belly and demonize it. Even Carl Gottlieb, who cowrote the screenplay, ignores the subtext. In *The Jaws Log*, he writes:

> Another steamy subplot that had been excised in creating the movie was the love affair between the police chief's wife and the young oceanographer. The sexual tension created by that liaison had been eliminated in favor of a more straightforward approach to the storytelling, an uncomplicated man-against-shark monster/adventure yarn with overtones of social conscience and individual action for the common good throughout.

Every summer, James asks me the same question: Why am I so fearful of and obsessed with sharks? After watching these movies, I begin to think my fascination is in direct proportion to my preoccupation with ideas of sentimental, obsessive, unrequited, and true love. The hopes and dreams I've held around love have an oblique counterpoint. My dread of sharks is my fear of loneliness, vulnerability, violence at the hands of something physically stronger, unemotional (and hungry). Also in the wings is the fantasy of submission, the danger of longing to be consumed by something strange.

Shark attacks are anthropomorphized crimes of passion, even divorce. The negative appetites that are attributed to sharks—greed, compulsion, cold-blooded ambition, violence, gluttony—are human vices. We all have savage sides and gaping maws, we all are capable of eating and being eaten. Even the language of love is destructive: Love will tear us apart. First the crush, being swept away, inflamed, devastated, consumed. *L'il shakin', l'il tenderizin', down ya go.*

Simply admitting that you're looking for love means accepting that you want to enter something that can bear you up and break your heart, means disrobing and getting in.

In giving up the laps, the control, and the reward system that swimming used to represent, I know that I should do the same with my marriage; that as much as I need to maintain it and pay attention to its currents and riptides, it's not something to win, not a course of known length with smooth, clear lanes. It is my small, open body of water, and if I'm careful, it may sustain me.

James and I spend a couple of nights in Prouts Neck, Maine, in a house once owned by Winslow Homer. Like Edward Hopper and Andy Warhol, Homer began his career as an illustrator, then moved on to the deeper wells of fine art. I think of illustration as a version of what we understand already, and in most cases we choose to be attracted to and see, whereas art reveals something we haven't yet seen, that hasn't yet been articulated, at least not in a familiar way.

Much of Homer's work hews to the conventions of illustration, but it gets interesting, to me, when it includes sharks. Next to his seaside pastorals and rocky shorelines, his fisherwomen and bathers, his few shark pieces stand out. In *The Gulf Stream*, painted in 1899, a lone black sailor reclines in a keeling boat, circled by sharks, a hurricane approaching, a frigate in the distance. *Sharks (The Derelict),* painted fourteen years earlier, shows a listing empty boat beset by writhing sharks, one of which, belly exposed, tips the boat precariously.

Both are strange, dreadful images, one of a man stuck

between unlikely salvation and gruesome death, the other of a lonely hull left to the ravages of nature. The weirdly passive and aggressive postures of the sharks in *Sharks* resemble the hapless orphan boy and the predator in *Watson and the Shark*, John Singleton Copley's dramatic 1778 depiction of Brook Watson, a fourteen-year-old crew member of a trading ship being attacked by a shark as men in a small boat struggle to save him.

Watson is naked, throat exposed, back arched, arm flung desperately toward the men, helpless and doomed. You see the desperation in the eyes of his rescuers, the cold gaping mouth of the shark, teeth glinting. Watson's posture is vulnerable and sexually ecstatic. (In the end, Watson lost part of his right leg, but survived to become Lord Mayor of London in 1796.)

Homer's and Copley's shark-subject paintings were their most enduring. In 2007, *Gulf Stream* and *Watson and the Shark* were installed at the Metropolitan Museum of Art alongside Damien Hirst's tiger shark in formaldehyde. The title that Hirst gave his 1991 piece is weirdly tender: *The Physical Impossibility of Death in the Mind of Someone Living*. Like Benchley, Hirst tries to circumlocate the unbearable. It's the shark that dare not speak its name: love.

VALS

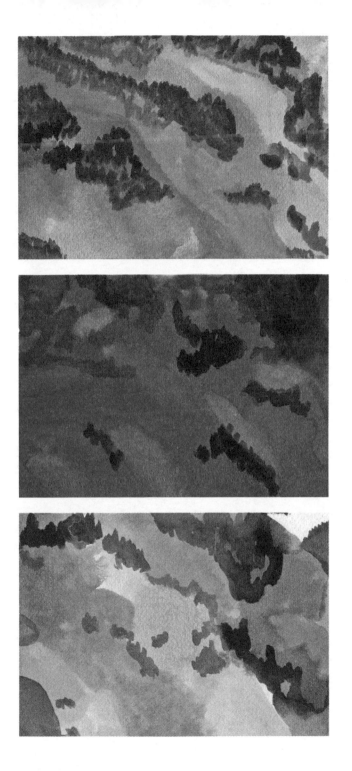

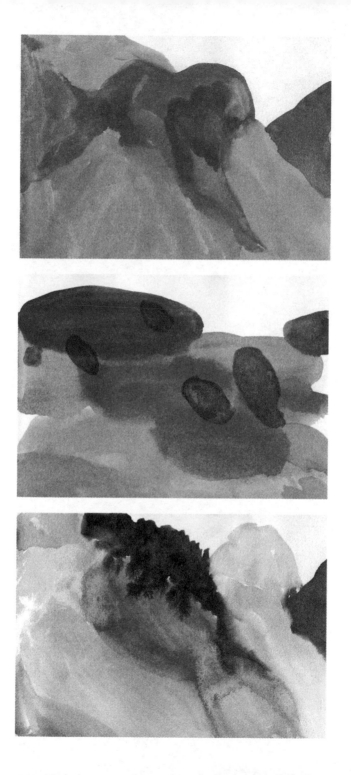

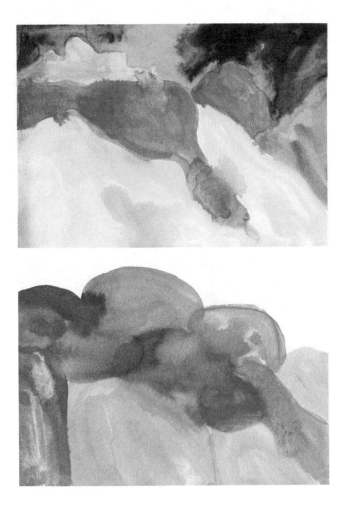

BATHING

The title of the book is *Zweminrichtingen: Swimming Pools*. A sticker on the back shows that it was purchased from David Mirvish Books on Art in Toronto. It is a pale-green-jacketed collection of black-and-white photographs of thirty Dutch swimming pools by Daria Scagliola, published in 1991. The photos I pause at are of the public pools, built in the 1930s or earlier. They are unpopulated, tiled neatly, signage—in tidy block type—visible at the water's edge. Other photographs are of abandoned outdoor pools, weeds sprouting between concrete tiles, water levels disturbingly low; it is like seeing a section of unshaven leg, or an abandoned drink. As I linger over these images I think of the ghosts of northern European swimmers and summers past, vaguely of the Second World War.

When I received this book in 1997, the Dutch pools, shot in the cool, sharp style of the Bernd and Hilla Becher school, gave me a missing perspective on my identity as a swimmer;

they provided some romance and distance, and addressed my artistic-mindedness more than cotton sweatshirts had. The inscription reads: *"Leanne, you spoke about this book once. I hope it's the right one or I'm a fool. The other half of the gift is unlimited use of a swimming pool in Ajax. A pool where you would swim as gracefully as I hope to be on the dance floor. Merry Christmas '97. Love Brendan."*

In his book *Gold in the Water: The True Story of Ordinary Men and Their Dream of Olympic Glory*, P. H. Mullen follows a team of Southern California swimmers preparing for the 2000 Olympics. One of them, Tate Blahnik, is a moody lone wolf of a swimmer whom Mullen describes as a self-loathing questioner of authority. He is described as possessing the most natural talent on the team, but is a reluctant champion, the athlete who hates practice. I think he's the most fascinating character in the book. The others, the ones who say and feel all the right things, are predictable. But they *do* win. Blahnik misses the Olympic team by a margin and is relieved to end his swimming career. Perhaps my sympathy for the might-have-been is a sour grapevine, but my admiration for and curiosity about athletes who are not goodwill motivational ambassadors is eternal.

In *The Fast and the Furious*, Alex Baumann, sidelined by a shoulder injury, explains that he hates missing practice:

"It's really hard watching a workout when you can't be in the pool," he monotones.

The narrator explains that Baumann wants to be a career diplomat.

Victor Davis, on the other hand, charismatically delivers a picture of discomfort and sacrifice:

"You get very tired and depressed, and you wish you had the social life that a lot of your friends have, you wish you could go out with this girl, but it's so hard to have that. You're too tired. . . . You wake up and your alarm goes off at five, and you just, you just *hear* the snow blowing outside, and you're in a nice warm waterbed and you say, I don't wanna go out there. Who wants to dive into water at five o'clock in the morning?"

Davis, the narrator explains, wants to be a policeman.

Later in the documentary, Davis finishes a disappointing second to Steve Lundquist in the 100m breaststroke at the 1982 World Championships. The camera watches Davis talk to his coach, Cliff, on deck. They go over the race, shaking their heads. Cliff sighs and says, "What can you do?" Davis mumbles almost inaudibly, "Go back and destroy the room." Cliff shakes his head. "You can't do that."

It reminds me of when Serena Williams's sweetie-pie demeanor falls away to reveal extreme aggression, reveals what anyone under that much pressure, pulling that much focus, determination, and desire, is concealing: a mind-boggling amount of coiled energy, gnashing. Why do we expect world-class athletes to always be polite and genial?

Characters like John Cheever's swimmer Neddy Merrill, Don DeLillo's blocker Gary Harkness, and David Foster Wallace's tennis prodigy Hal Incandenza illuminate a wider, more complicated swath of culture by not winning. Their swims, games, matches aren't redemptive. Their trajectories don't set up victory.

I watch YouTube footage of races, documentaries like *The Fast and the Furious, Michael Phelps: Inside Story of the Beijing Games*, and *Unfiltered: Michael Phelps & Ian Crocker—The Story Behind the Rivalry*, and while I could replay Jason Lezak's 2008 4x100m freestyle relay finish for hours, the parts I find most touching are the interiors, the kitchens, the glasses of milk, a swimmer eating dinner from a plate set atop a television set, lamplight, parents, teal duvets, socks on staircases, and carpeted hallways.

I'm a poorly drawn jock. I suspect, these days, I am more suited to bathing.

Bathing implies having some contact with the ground while in the water—propulsion and speed are secondary. Bathing. *Bathing:* the word itself feels like a balm, a cleanse, rather than the wavy struggle of *swimming*. I wonder why swimming in North America feels different from swimming in Europe.

Until the late seventeenth century, the sea was regarded as a place of danger and death, the aspect of houses was directed inland, sailors were not taught to swim, in order to foster in them a true respect for the sea. The ocean stank, was dangerous, belched up seaweed and flotsam, and was full of marauding pirates and monsters. The value of any coast-line was in proportion to how fortified it was. Swimming instruction as military drill for men and horses began in the late eighteenth and early nineteenth centuries in northern Europe, accompanying developments in toilets and indoor plumbing.

In *The Springboard in the Pond: An Intimate History of the Swimming Pool*, Thomas A. P. van Leeuwen talks about the impression physical activity made on European visitors to the United States in the 1890s: "Americans seem best to express their spiritual energy by moving their bodies, by running, walking fast, and competing in sports."

I think of the only time my medals have come in handy, at the U.S. border crossing in Buffalo. As Jason and I pull up at the border after inching through a traffic jam from Toronto, a guard eyes us suspiciously and asks for our passports. We look a mess; the car reeks of B.O. and chicken nuggets. Vintage clothes are strewn across the backseat, moth-eaten blankets lumpily cover Jason's camera equipment. One of my father's art-college paintings is jammed between our luggage. I'm certain we'll be pulled over to the side, as I often am, and interrogated. The guard gets out of his booth and asks me to pop the back. I do. Shuffling sounds, then: "Who's the swimmer?" I smile at Jason. "I am." The hatchback shuts quietly. The guard hands us our passports with no further questions, just "Drive safely." Before I left my parents' house I heaved a large tote bag into the car; in it were eight years' worth of gold, silver, and bronze swimming medals.

While visiting Berlin, I meet an artist who swims every morning, so I ask him about the city's pools. He quickly makes a list of those he likes in my notebook. His daily laps are done at Stadtbad Mitte, in Gartenstrasse.

I head first to Stadtbad Charlottenburg–Alte Halle, a small, pretty pool nestled in the leafy streets of western Berlin. I borrow a pair of children's goggles from the lifeguard booth and swim short widths beside a thick red rope bisecting the pool. A labored mural of Hylas and the Nymphs overlooks the deep end. The pool is beautiful but feels heavily furnished, like a parlor. The other swimmers seem to be annoyed by my splashing.

Stadtbad Mitte, completed in 1930, is a soaring, gridded glass box. It is bright and unusually airy for a pool, thanks to its high mullioned transparent roof. (In 1945 its roof was struck by two Allied bombs—conceivably dropped by my grandfather or some friends of his—that failed to explode.) The deck is tiled in small pale gray squares; there are slurping gutters along the sides, two staircases that lead to a very shallow end, and a three-foot drop from the deck to the water's surface that makes the pool feel contained, tanklike. There are only eight other swimmers, most doing relaxed but steady laps. In the deep end I sink to the bottom and look around. The swimmers glide calmly overhead, my bubbles rise, glittering. I push off the bottom.

In Bath, England, for a literary festival, I visit the ancient Roman baths. Usually, any ruin filled with algae-greened water thrills me, but as I walk through the boxy displays and past the projected re-creations of "Romans" wearing too much mascara, I am bored. Even the two-thousand-year-old skeleton with cavities from eating honey does nothing for me. The statues the Victorians erected around the terrace overlooking the large outdoor pool upstage the real Roman stonework, the bath's cruder but authentic roots. What I love, however, are the Roman curse tablets: tiny outrages scratched into pieces of lead and pewter and nailed to the wall, requesting that the gods visit misfortune on the heads of whoever stole their stuff while they were swimming. One reads:

> To Minerva the goddess of Sulis I have given the thief who has stolen my hooded cloak, whether slave or free, whether man or woman. He is not to buy back this gift unless with his own blood.

I could relate, remembering the time my coral-pink Club Monaco sweatshirt was stolen from the Clarkson pool women's locker room when I was thirteen. One minute I belonged to The Club of Monaco. Then suddenly I didn't. My father was furious at the theft; on the chilly drive home his incredulity at my trust in other children vibrated in the car. I cursed the girl who had taken it.

Walking along the uneven, original deck of the Great Bath is more interesting; the sky overhead is cloudy, and the murky green water is steaming. At one corner James crouches and sticks his hand into the pool, ignoring the many "Do Not Touch the Water As It Is Untreated" signs.

"Toasty," he says.

I look around, then do the same. He's right. I wipe my fingers on my pant leg and we exit, heading for tea in the Pump Room. I wash my hands before picking up my finger sandwiches, but James doesn't bother. I think about ancient Roman germs while he butters his raisin-studded Bath bun.

The following day we visit the Thermae Bath Spa behind the Roman baths, a modern facility fed by the original hot springs. In its film and image archive, the Thermae website presents black-and-white footage from the 1960s and 1970s of middle-aged men and women floating in the old pools with the aid of rubber doughnut-shaped inflatables. The water is cloudy, surrounded by age-stained stonework and white tiles. A color clip shows a feature film being shot in the great Roman bath: actors in buttercup-yellow tunics enter the green steaming water, as directed by a bearded man with a megaphone. In another, a woman is lowered by a system of ropes and pulleys into a dark pool, where a therapist waits to gently open and close her legs. In the films, the slightly mildewed old pools look beautiful. Traces of amoebic meningitis were found in the waters in the 1970s, necessitating the closing of the baths.

We buy a ticket for a two-hour session and enter the Thermae spa. After changing we head to the Minerva pool on the lower level. The pool, amoeba-shaped, is vast, bright blue, and filled with middle-aged men and women. I'm surprised by the number of adults clutching blue pool-noodles beneath their armpits. A group of bathers congregate in a submerged whirlpool area at one end, voices raised over the bubbling water. James and I swim around self-consciously. The pool is chlorinated, the room is loud, and I wonder bleakly how many people have peed in the very warm water, relying on the chlorine to absolve and absorb their relief. We kick to the side and go in search of the steam rooms.

A few months later I'm in Switzerland. I float toward and rest my elbows on the third step of a flight of shallow stairs that descend into the deeper water of the pool beneath and behind me. My knees hover above the fifth step. It is eleven-fifteen p.m. The reflection of two tiny orange dock lights breaks and shimmers before me in the water of the *Aussenbad*, the outdoor pool at Hotel Therme Vals, a Swiss hotel with a spa designed by Peter Zumthor that opened in 1996.

I resolved to swim in these pools someday, after seeing photographs of the spa on a design blog. While not usually drawn to architecture, I was mesmerized by the pictures of the Vals pools. I bookmarked the page, and kept returning to it to study the dark granite layers of the walls, the clean tectonic structure, the gleaming, dimly lit pools. Externally, the spa is concealed by the slope of the mountainside, the *Aussenbad* visible only from the air. The interiors have the mysterious appeal of caverns without the cartoon interruption of stalagmite and stalactite.

A light steam floats up and above the surface of the water.

Speaking is forbidden. These silent night swims are offered Sundays, Wednesdays, and Thursdays to hotel guests. The dark quiet and the architecture reduce us to blots on a grid, our bobbing round heads like single musical notes in Zumthor's composition.

I get into the water as soon as we arrive, elated. The water is kept at thirty degrees Celsius in the summer, easy to enter without a flinch. I wade down the first set of steps and push off in a glide down a high, narrow corridor and through a low chain curtain in a glass wall that separates indoor and outdoor space. The day is overcast, making the water gray and raising a light fog across the surface. I swim over to three periscoping brass spouts, each pouring a strong stream of water, and stand under one. I let the water pummel my shoulders, then kick around the perimeter of the pool. I sit, shoulders submerged, on each of its three shallow staircases—one leading straight into a wall. After floating, gazing, and kicking around, I swim back inside to try the *Eisbad*, a tiny pebble-bottomed pool kept at fourteen degrees Celsius. I can stay in only long enough to plunge, then head straight for the *Feuerbad*, kept at forty-two degrees Celsius. I explore each space and pool: a perfumed pool filled with flower petals; a series of three steam rooms with smooth marble tablets the size of sarcophagi, spotlit by amber light; a warm-water warren that eventually situates you in the bottom of a towering cube, like a conceptual modernist dungeon.

Finally I enter the large *Innenbad*, glimmering beneath a grid of small blue glass skylights. The pool is closing in twenty minutes and emptying out. I am alone but for one other woman, in a striped bikini. Sliding along a submerged bar on one wall I look up just in time to see her floating backward toward a copper handrail. I call out, but her ears are underwater and she bangs her head sharply on the pole.

In water, most of the communication is physical. I like being so close to strangers' bodies, seeing their clumsiness and vulnerability. In the *Feuerbad*, one man looks deeply uncomfortable, exposed in his trunks; a woman whose compact body suggests former gymnast chomps on gum. I float behind an older couple who don't get their heads wet, who trail the scent of dusty perfume and car. Women wear swimsuits that are too big or too small, men's muscles appear tender and extreme.

I wake, cranky, from holiday naps, but the hotel's complex of pools and steam rooms in the hill below its rooms calms me. The design evokes the sensation of flying: once inside the pools, instead of feeling at the surface of things, Zumthor's towering layers of stone walls make it feel as though I'm moving through the earth-bound spaces, hallways and corners, courtyards and rooms. Most pool architecture surrounds the water in horizontal planes—he's done the opposite, surrounding his pools with stacked verticals, making the water an element to float atop, rather than sink into. The effect is dreamlike, weightless. As though, in the midst of heavy rocks, jammed beneath mountains, our own corporeal weight is overwhelmed, negated.

During the silent night swim, couples enter the water and look around, gravitating bodily toward each other, exchanging nods and caresses. The affectionate float into each other's faces, touch each other's heads, cradling, bumping, and holding each other lightly. The postures are passive, of surrender, chins, necks exposed. As they support each other to float on their backs, the bathers drop into a voluntary, light pietà, a gesture submissive and gorgeous.

It reminds me of learning mouth-to-mouth resuscitation. How we were taught to tip the neck back and pinch the nose to open the airway, a profile that still fills me with alarm. Half of the class would be sent, shivering, to the pool office or locker room, then summoned a few minutes later to find the other half of the class in simulated emergency situations. One person would be on the bottom of the pool, another flailing by a ladder. There would always be a bleeding cut, a head wound, someone passed out on the tiles, and a couple of panicked swimmers in the deep end screaming that they didn't know how to swim. We'd rush toward the victims, our lifesaving techniques overseen by instructors, some insisting on a "full seal," others okay with a few centimeters of space between lips. I can clearly remember two of my classmates, one dripping boy bent purposefully over on his knees, his breath inflating the cheeks of the other flat on his back, their lips rubbery and slick.

Between my thrice-daily swims, I paint the view from my window twenty-three times. Our room is on the top floor and looks over the valley and the tiny town of Vals. From the room next to ours I hear a couple laughing hysterically, the woman's laugh high and shrieking, the man's wobbly and low. The laughter turns into low Swiss-German conversation, then laughter again, and finally the man sighs a loud, trembling sigh that falls as he exhales with a happy wheeze and all goes quiet.

On our last day I get up to make it to the pool when it opens at seven. A few people are there already: a woman, dry, sitting and staring at the pool, her legs drawn up to her chest; another woman in the *Aussenbad*, her eyes a picture of suspicion and surprise; a couple swaddled in white robes identical to mine. As I float around, more swimmers arrive. A middle-aged woman with a modern haircut gracefully enters the water: Duchamp's not-quite-nude descending a staircase. Three old men do steady laps of breaststroke in the longest part of the pool. On my way back to the *Innenbad*, I pass the dry woman, still sitting with her legs drawn up to her chest, still staring at the water.

We are all aware of one another. As on a dance floor, I'll try out someone else's moves while others imitate mine. I see a couple hook their feet over a bar and float on their backs; I do the same and experience a strange, head-heavy weightlessness, not unpleasant but unsettling, body weight collecting in my neck and shoulders. I lie lengthwise along a shallow shelf, my body just submerged, and a man watches and then does the same. Mid-morning an attendant navigates a Zamboni-like contraption past me. It sucks up the puddles on the shining slate, leaving a dry, matte surface behind. I get out and walk in its wake, making darker gray prints on the stone.

SWIMMING POOLS

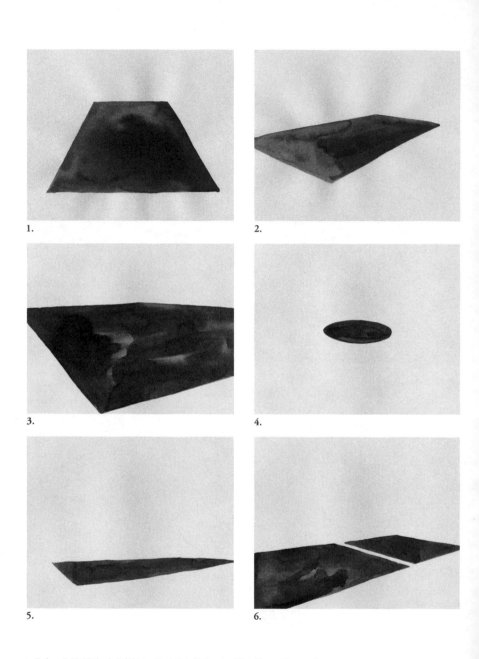

1. Robert J. H. Kiphuth Exhibition Pool, Yale University, New Haven, Connecticut
2. Roosevelt Hotel, Hollywood, California
3. Baruch College Athletics and Recreation Complex, New York City
4. Jamaica Inn, Ocho Rios, Jamaica
5. Sheraton Centre, Toronto
6. Etobicoke Olympium, Etobicoke, Ontario

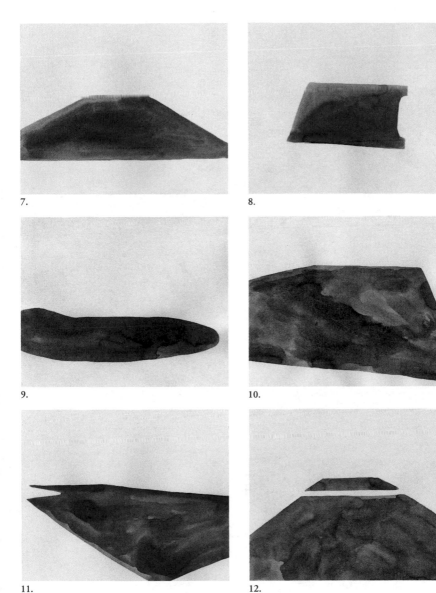

7. West Side YMCA, New York City
8. Riad Mabrouka, Fès, Morocco
9. Hotel Beverly Terrace, Los Angeles
10. Metropolitan Recreation Center, Williamsburg, Brooklyn, New York
11. UCLA Sunset Canyon Recreation Center, Los Angeles
12. Université de Sherbrooke, Sherbrooke, Quebec

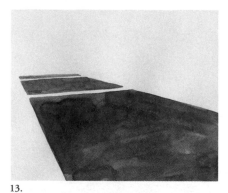

13.

14.

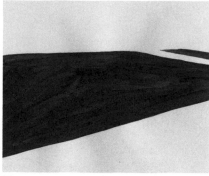

15.

16.

17.

18.

13. Asphalt Green (Upper East Side), New York City
14. Fitness First, Baker Street, London
15. Highbury Pool, London
16. Serson Pool, Mississauga, Ontario
17. Barbados Aquatic Centre, Barbados
18. Foster Pool, Lakewood, Ohio

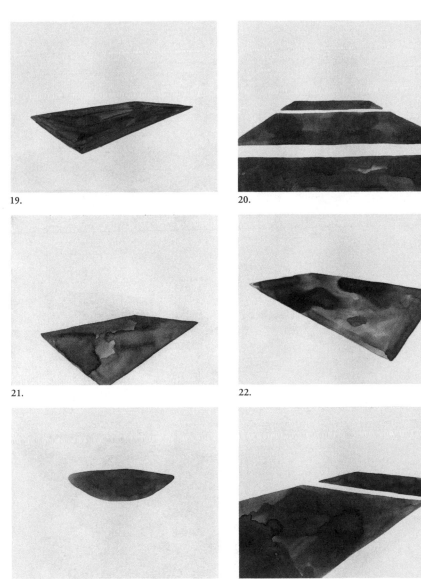

19.

20.

21.

22.

23.

24.

19. Holiday Inn City West, Berlin
20. Wayne Gretzky Sports Centre, Brantford, Ontario
21. Holiday Inn Express & Suites, Minneapolis
22. Cawthra Pool, Mississauga, Ontario
23. Thermae Bath Spa rooftop pool, Bath, England
24. Pan Am Pool, Winnipeg, Manitoba

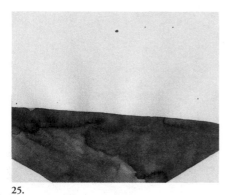

25.

26.

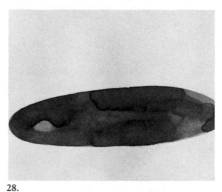

27.

28.

29.

30.

25. Edmonton Kinsmen Sports Centre, Edmonton, Alberta
26. Terry Fox Memorial Pool, Mississauga, Ontario
27. Stadtbad Mitte, Berlin
28. Chateau Marmont, Los Angeles
29. Erin Meadows Pool, Mississauga, Ontario
30. Backyard pool, North Salem, New York

31.

32.

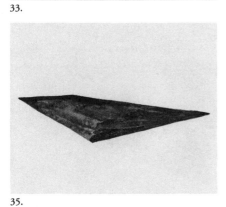

33.

34.

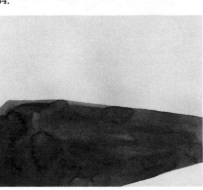

35.

36.

31. Manhattan Plaza Racquet Club, New York City
32. Meadowvale Pool, Mississauga, Ontario
33. Miraflores Park Hotel, Lima
34. *Innenbad,* Hotel Therme Vals, Switzerland
35. Babington House infinity pool, Somerset, England
36. Wilton Family Y, Wilton, Connecticut

37.

38.

39.

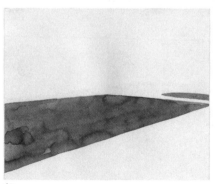

40.

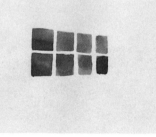

41.

42.

37. *Aussenbad,* Hotel Therme Vals, Switzerland
38. Centralbadet, Stockholm
39. Eleanor Misener Aquatic Centre, Brock University, St. Catharines, Ontario
40. Piscine de Pontoise, Paris
41. Le Westin Montréal, Montreal
42. Astoria Pool, Queens, New York

43.

44.

45.

46.

47.

48.

43. Backyard pool, Staatsburg, New York
44. Huron Park Recreation Centre, Mississauga, Ontario
45. Centennial Pool, Halifax, Nova Scotia
46. Riad des Golfs, Agadir, Morocco
47. Villa pool, Goat Hill, Jamaica
48. The Berkeley, London

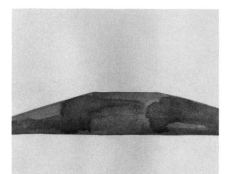

49.

50.

51.

52.

53.

54.

49. Glenforest Pool, Mississauga, Ontario
50. Claremont Hotel Club & Spa, Berkeley, California
51. Çırağan Palace Kempinski, Istanbul
52. Oasis Sports Centre, London
53. Laugardalslaug, Reykjavík
54. Villa Buonvisi, Lucca, Italy

55.

56.

57.

58.

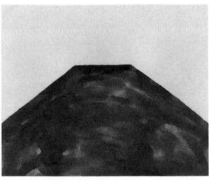

59.

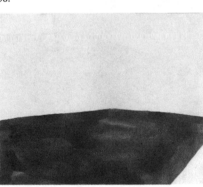

60.

55. Round Hill Hotel & Villas, Hopewell, Jamaica
56. Piscine du Parc Olympique, Montreal
57. Backyard pool, Ajax, Ontario
58. Venetian, Las Vegas
59. Jeno Tihanyi Olympic Gold Pool, Laurentian University, Sudbury, Ontario
60. Nay Aug Park, Scranton, Pennsylvania

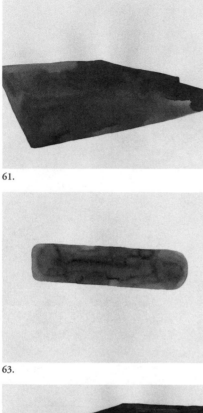

61.

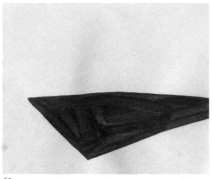

62.

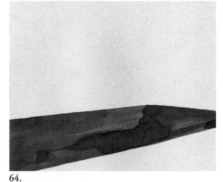

64.

65.

66.

63.

61. Four Seasons, Toronto
62. Memorial Pool, McGill University, Montreal
63. Sunnyside–Gus Ryder Pool, Toronto
64. Nepean Sportsplex, Ottawa
65. Château Laurier, Ottawa
66. University of Toronto Athletic Centre, Toronto

67.

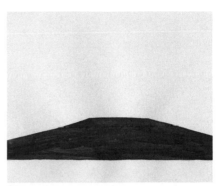

68.

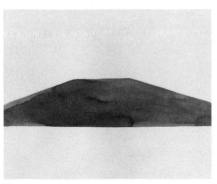

69.

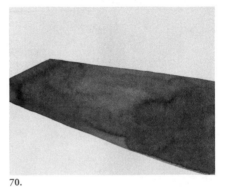

70.

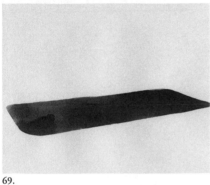

71.

67. King Pool, Berkeley, California
68. Clarkson Pool, Mississauga, Ontario
69. Backyard pool, Gaucin, Spain
70. McBurney YMCA, New York City
71. Stadtbad Charlottenburg–Alte Halle, Berlin

SECOND SWIM

On a cold November morning, I drive my rented Ford Focus to the Etobicoke Olympium to watch the preliminary heats of a national meet.

I sit with Linda and Byron. After their heats the swimmers clamber into the stands, arms full of clothes and towels, cap and goggles tucked into their suits, and confer with their coaches. The swimmers breathe hard, staring, nodding, faces slack while they listen for something that will either reassure or congratulate. They ask whether they swam well enough to get a second swim, in other words, if they are in the top sixteen, which means a chance to race in the evening final.

The latest technical suits are constricting and unbearable to wear for much longer than fifteen minutes. Between races, the women pull on training suits and yank their competition suit straps under their armpits before heading to the warm-down pool, or wear sports bras, keeping the tight suits at their hips. As I take notes, a swimmer beside me tucks a towel around his waist, and in a wiggling, pretzel-twisting matter of seconds, he has completely changed into his street clothes.

Byron tells me a little bit about some of the better swimmers, stories of crazy parents, interteam love affairs, and burnout rates, I remark that when I swam with him at the University of Toronto I didn't know half as much about my teammates.

"Well, you were a bit of an outsider. You lived off campus, and you didn't go to the parties. There are a lot of hours to fill at those varsity parties, you know."

I nod, decide not to mention I wasn't invited.

"You sit down next to someone at a party, they're going to tell you a few things."

When I ask, Byron tells me about his own trajectory. After finishing sixth in the 100m butterfly at the 1972 Munich Olympics, he considered retiring, as most Olympians did after one Games. He explains that there are swimmers who do well because they love the sport, and swimmers who do well because they are talented; that though he had natural talent—his stroke was described as "near perfect"—he was one of the former. He stresses it is the love of the sport and training that elevates some swimmers above others. He likes to paraphrase something a baseball manager once said: "Swimming is my soul. I live it twenty-four hours a day and love it."

Instead of retiring, Byron swam for another four years, enjoying the travel opportunities, though missing placement on the 1976 Olympic Team. He had a degree in commerce from the University of Michigan, but eased seamlessly into coaching on the basis of his reputation as a swimmer.

"Most coaches were high school teachers back then," he says, shrugging. "There were only a handful of good coaches in the country."

After prelims, I leave the bleachers and wander past a table selling plain hoodies, sweatshirts, and T-shirts. Next to the table is a rack of track pants, and flannel pajama bottoms covered in ladybugs, flowers, paw prints. On the walls and tabletop are a variety of heat transfers available to iron onto the clothing.

The messages range from the challenging—*I've been training mine off so I can kick yours; YES I'm a girl, YES I'm a swimmer, YES I'll kick your butt; I CAN FLY, What's Your Superpower?*—to the defensive—*Swimming is my life, DEAL WITH IT; Real swimmers don't make excuses, they make waves; If swimming were any easier, it would be called hockey*—to the inspirational monotone—*Veni, Natavi, Vici, I came, I swam, I conquered; Canadian Swimmers Rule;* and simply: *I Love Swimming.*

The phrases look like bumper stickers, fonts of flirty italic and collegiate block, in palettes of pink, blue, and lime green. It is very assertive. It makes me apprehensive, but it is the language of belonging.

I look at the flannel pajama bottoms, pull out a pair of mauve ones covered in red ladybugs and white daisies. I wonder where I would wear them. The man behind the table tells me the hot-pink transfer would look good on them. He lays the fat word *SWIMMING* along one leg. I tell the man I will think about it.

I walk away, seriously thinking about it, into the small pro shop across the hall. The walls are covered with flippers, pull buoys, caps, and goggles. Kickboards and nylon duffels sit high on shelves; a glass counter displays chamois, Swedish goggles, and special swimmers' shampoo.

Along one wall hang the bathing suits. The styles have changed since 1992. There are now endurance suits made of thicker material, bright training suits in psychedelic digital prints with thin straps and cutaway backs, competition suits in slick polyester blends, water-repellent fabrics with bonded seams and compression panels. I run my fingers along the suits. My heat transfer would say: *I Put the Longing in Belonging*. I consider a swimsuit in a blue-and-green tartan pattern. I think of how itchy a woven wool tartan swimsuit would be.

Leaving the pool parking lot, I make a left into the wide street, heading for the highway. I can't figure out the satellite radio dial, so I give up and let sound tracks choose me.

Gordon Lightfoot: "Sundown." Genesis: "Follow You."

It is overcast. The sedate landscape of bungalow housing and convenience plaza closes around my heart. My thinking is mushy again, my heat transfer reads: *Home Is Where the Heart Is*. I miss an exit and drive beneath several underpasses and along an airport service road, eventually finding my way back to a familiar street, recognizing the buff-colored apartment complex where my grandmother first lived after immigrating to Canada from the Philippines in 1974. Where she'd feed me homemade sugar doughnuts and fried plantains.

I think of why I left swimming, left Toronto, left Canada. I know there are two sides, two lives, feel them acutely, not athlete and adult, but the life of the body and the life of the heart.

I think about loving swimming the way you love somebody. How a kiss happens, gravitational. About compromise, sacrifice, and breakup. The heart can suffer more than a few not-quites, have poor timing. We are outtouched by others, can psych ourselves out, we lose, win, become our results, find our place and rank.

I think about loving swimming the way you love a country. The backseat of my father's car, driving through Toronto's older neighborhoods to see the Christmas lights. Framed photographs of a twenty-six-year-old Queen Elizabeth above classroom blackboards, ill-fitting wool coats and fur coats, ice-skate exchanges. A community center pool parking lot at four fifty-five a.m., where sleet makes the sound of brushed steel against a car door. A frozen rope clangs against a flagpole. (The door to the far left is unlocked; inside, warm, the pool lights flicker on in bays.) Ever present is the smell of chlorine, and the drifting of snow in the dark.

ACKNOWLEDGMENTS

Thank you, Ken Whyte, Michael Schmelling, Byron Mac-Donald, Sarah Hochman, Helen Conford, Anna Jardine, Jason Fulford, Miranda Purves, Mark Lotto, Sheila Heti, Kylie Minor, Deirdre Dolan, Craig Taylor, Lorin Stein, Sara Angel, Friederike Schilbach, Richard McGuire, Mary Robertson, Mary Duenwald, Deborah Moggach, David Shipley, Andrew Wylie, Sarah Chalfant, Luke Ingram, Rebecca Nagel, Pamela Baguley, Susanne Kippenberger, Niklas Maak, Ben Schott, Greg Weir, Mitch Ivey, François Laurin, Jim McMullan, USMS, Erin Sulpher and Melissa Sweet at Swimming Canada. Great love and thanks to James Truman, and deepest gratitude to my family, Lorna, Bob, and Derek Shapton.